Anger Management for Parents

The Ultimate Guide to Positive Parenting Without Anger. Perfect for Emotion Control, Learn Effective Communication for New and Experienced Parents

Henry Hal

CONSIDER BEST WAY TO REACT
RELAX AND STAY CALM
TAKE DEEP BREATHS
COUNT TO 10
EXERCISE
KEEP JOURNAL
TALK TO SOMEONE
TELL YOURSELF YOU ARE RIGHT
MANAGING ANGER

TABLE OF CONTENTS

Introduction

Individuals, groups and seminars concerned with child management and anger management are encouraged to utilize the book. therapists, group leaders, and individual readers can feel free to study the chapters in whatever sequence best suits their requirements because each chapter stands on its own.

The opening chapter of the book, Chapter 1, is strongly recommended for those who are studying the book alone. It provides information about anger in general, as well as a method of examining how anger develops through time.

The majority of lessons include exercises that will assist you in understanding and changing your habits in order to benefit your family and children. Each exercise begins with real-life examples that serve as both a guide and a model for how to complete the exercise properly and effectively. The more you put out effort in these exercises, the more likely it is that you will create rewarding changes in your family life. You will begin to view anger for what it truly is: a burden.

We strongly advise you to keep a private diary or journal while making your way through the book. Examples of how to document accomplishments in making real-life changes are provided at the conclusion of most lessons. It will be extremely beneficial for you to keep track of good changes since it will aid you in maintaining your efforts and making a long-term impact in your life and the lives of your children.

We all want the best for our children and want to be the greatest parents perfect for them. It's possible that you have a propensity to judge yourself as a terrible parent when you lose your temper or otherwise fall short of your ideal. Please be patient and tolerant with yourself as you attempt to implement the real-world changes advised in this article. We are all perfect individuals. On every lengthy trip, we must begin with little steps in the correct direction. It is possible to make progress by taking two steps forward and one step back. Make use of the information provided here as a map that you may reference to choose the direction you desire to move in and to take the initial steps. Getting even a little portion of the way there will make a significant impact for you and your family.

Chapter 1

THE ANGER CHAIN

Wrath is about control. Many parents are caught trying to control their children, therefore filling their families with anger. As it happens, the parents are more frustrated and depressed, while the children are more remote and often out of control.

It is useful to understand how and why, once planted in the family, anger tends to develop in intensity and regularity. Like an addictive substance, intense wrath is needed and demanded more often to satisfy the habits of wrath.

First, a difference concerning the words of anger:

Others do not see our furious thoughts or feelings, therefore we ask for these inner occurrences to prepare for angry behaviour. These include sentiments of anger, offense, victimisation, vengeance plotting, thinking about the faults of others and the sensation of justified outrage.

Other individuals can observe our furious acts and displays so that they are labeled angry behaviours. These include wrathful facial expressions, wrathful remarks, threatening gestures, striking and murdering.

When a dad reacts with a sensation of rage to his son's poor lawn mowing, the dad's body prepares to physically assault his kid. The furious mood is actually his sensation of these inner bodily preparations, his physical knowledge of them. Chemicals in your body that accelerate your heart, provide greater blood flow to your arms and legs and increase blood pressure have been released. These bodily alterations tune the father's physique to assault his son physically.

It is frightening to consider in such basic terms about your sense of fury. We usually don't know that our sensation of rage is the preparation of our body to physically assault someone. We seldom ever perform a physical attack. Our wrathful acts usually tell the other person that we are about to assault them. That warning, taken seriously, is frequently enough to get us what we desire. Our facial expressions can be sufficient to have a youngster turn the radio down. If it is not enough, furious speech can work. And if it doesn't, we can yell threateningly at the youngster.

Regardless matter how skillfully we describe our parental anger as necessary and normal, any such furious conduct can be successful depending on children being treated as stages to physical damage. In other words, the efficacy of furious conduct depends on learning by the children to avoid what may follow. Effective parental rage must make children dread.

Furious sentiments and angry behaviours, forming a chain that extends from small irritations with accompanying facial grimaces to an all-out physical attack, have a sense of fury. Once parents start to feel furious with their children, they tend to travel to the extreme end of the anger chain.

Making and Enforcing Rules

As parents, we aim to nurture, protect, educate and welcome young people into our society. We all know that without rules we cannot live together in a civilized way. We are all aware of the necessity for regulations for children. But what is a rule and what is the aim of parenthood?

Do we establish rules for children to be controlled? If you believe that your duty as a parent is to manage your kid, your usage of rules is an attempt to control it. Control needs to be ready to punish, so you're ready to be furious. Control means "making" someone to do something and sooner or later it is always the largest stick, the strongest menace and a readiness to use threats to create fear.

Susan sees regulations as a tool to get John to do what she wants. John breaches her rules often. "Mow the yard every Friday before I come home, for instance." Every time John breaches her rules, Susan gets more and more upset. The harshness of his punishment is steadily increased. These penalties, given in fury, even when it settles down, appear severe to her. She backs down often.

If you regard regulations as a method to manage children, violating rules will be increasingly harmful. And if youngsters continue to violate the rules, they are more harmed. Your control theory requires that you create a scenario where alternatives to what you want to accomplish are so unpleasant that people opt to abide by your rules. For example, day after day at a school, they sit through boredom instead of skipping school, and then are grounded, punched, screamed at or worse.

Susan genuinely doesn't want to control John. She understands instinctively that successful controls would need his independence to be squashed. Susan loves his approach independently. But she doesn't know any option to punishing John for trying to control him.

Susan's John issue is prevalent today. Many parents understand that regulations are needed, but do not know how to apply them except with more harmful results. The repercussions are often "promised" in wrath. Because they are too severe to do, save in fury, they are only performed in anger.

An alternative to utilizing child control rules is to use rules to influence children's self-control. This calls for two changes that Susan and most parents do:

- The consequences for breaking a rule have to be the same each time the rule is broken to affect the self-control of youngsters.

- Regulatory enforcement should express the unchanging expectations of their parents with regard to children's behaviour. Therefore, when rules are broken, parents must be there to illustrate those expectations by implementing them.

We shall leave the difficulty in this chapter till later. It generally includes careful consideration of the economic and lifestyle objectives of the parent. Susan enjoys good things, for example, costly clothing, vehicles, houses and furniture. She still does not comprehend that the time to acquire these items is not their only expense. Their effect on John's self-control cost less time with John.

Parents may feel that regulations must be constantly enforced in order to be effective. But they don't. But they don't. What is overlooked is that the implementation must be the same every time a rule is broken in order to be consistent. The reason behind this is that:

- If a parent sees rules as a method of controlling the conduct of a kid, then the parent considers the rule faulty each time the rule is tested (breached). The youngster wasn't controlled.

- They're right. They're correct. If rules are to govern behavior, violating the rule implies that it did not function. A tougher rule is needed – one that hurts the youngster more.

- If the function of parent rules is not the management of children by parents but the control of themselves by children, the penalties of violation of rules must be same each time.

- The rules are designed to teach our children of our unwavering expectations for their behavior, just as natural laws influence their behavior by having constant results. When youngsters crash against a wall, it always has the same impact. Children are not under control; they are influenced to govern themselves. They're using the door.

Inconsistency in applying rules weakens their help to the sense of safety and self-control of children much as the barriers sometimes allow them to pass through and sometimes do not confuse and terrify them. Children do not know what their future behaviour will be automatically. If we think that one day they will live and prosper in a civilized culture, we must teach our children about our faith in their future. Rules assist us to achieve it if they are consistent with principles. If they fluctuate and the effects alter, while we go all over the place while children are misbehaving, then rules are anything but certain expectations. This reveals regulations as parental attempts to regulate the conduct of the kid.

Using Our Own Unhappiness to Control Children

Wrath is about control. Its aim is to make someone feel awful if they don't do what they desire. Any technique to make somebody feel awful may therefore become an instrument of rage and control. One convenient method to make our loved ones, even children, feel terrible is to prove that they harmed us.

If you demonstrate them they are accountable for harming you, you may make them feel awful. Being angry and appearing upset are strategies of controlling those who love you. It's normal for us to say to a loved one when they hurt us. "Ouch! Stop\ sthat." We rely on the other person who cares for our "touch." It is not control. It is not control. It tells them how their actions affect us.

Most kids love their parents much as their parents love them. They don't want their parents to do anything terrible. You will care for your parents as much as you can. Because kids care for their parents, they hurt if parents are sad or dissatisfied. You want your parents to feel well. This is the basis for parents' pleasure. Children like laughing and smiling at their parents. As a consequence:

- Being upset may become a kid control technique for parents.

- Being ready to get outraged over any unreasonable conduct of children may become a job for parents.

Mona thinks Jimmy's parenting role as addressing any misconduct. Her approach to discipline him is to be dissatisfied with him. So she became used to being prepared to be miserable. For his first twelve years, her misery was an excellent control method. It won't keep controlling him much longer. She won't lose her ability to make him feel awful. He will learn to feel unpleasant and unpleasant.

Mona feels this shift is going to happen, but she doesn't know how to stop it. Years ago, Jimmy's father escaped from their marriage. He couldn't continue to have so much sorrow in a woman whom he loved. Mona attempted every method she knew she was unhappy to bring him back, even in a serious attempt to commit suicide. The more pain she displayed towards the end of her relationship because of her departure, the more desperate he was to get away.

Jimmy shows indications of staying away as well. When he's with his mother, he's quieter. He doesn't come home immediately from school. He spends a lot of time in his room, even if the television and stereo are in the living room below.

Mona's response to the shifting conduct of Jimmy is to show further worry at his actions. This will lead him further away, leading her to become more concerned. As this cycle escalates, a pall spreads around the home shortly before her husband leaves.

To avoid what is ahead, Mona has to alter her belief in what brings her sorrow. She thinks that Jimmy makes her feel wretched. But misery is something that she exploits to dominate him in her endeavors. Mona tries to manage Jimmy by making him feel awful when he scares or dis-pleases her. She truly feels her spouse was unhappy, and her kid now follows suit. It will be very hard for her to relinquish her dissatisfaction. She feels that being happy means giving Jimmy license to do anything he wants. It appears to her that to give up unhappiness means to take an opportunity for Jimmy to abandon her. In fact, the contrary is true. Leaving him apart from her pain is the only way she can keep Jimmy near. She must give him the opportunity to love her freely.

It is absolutely worth using this opportunity for both of them. Not only is Mona losing her unhappiness, but she's going to acquire a son who spends time with her because he wants to be there. And Jimmy's going to get a happy parent. He won't bear the burden of his mother's unhappiness any more.

When we consider both rules and control — and now discomfort — as anger, it becomes evident that lowering parental anger entails important personal changes.

You can't go on as you were and merely push a magic button to create model kids.

There is a huge reward for eliminating the use of misfortune as a tool to dominate our loved ones. Getting rid of the misfortune that we utilize as rage gets rid of many of our misfortune.

If someone close to you hurts you, it is worth showing your grief to him or her. Unhappiness acts as communication in this situation. But much of our dissatisfaction is designed to attack, to control and to make another feel awful, especially as parents. Giving it up is releasing you from a thousand days of cloud.

Parents may discover themselves to be the "police of happiness." They might become the protectors of seriousness without recognizing it. Maybe you saw this happen to pals. Someone you knew was as prankster and good time Charlie as anybody else you met. You haven't seen the guy for a long and there could be an opportunity to get to know him again.

You might try playing and playing in the way you did when your two were kids. Your attempts to jest have a serious or even outraged answer. Your buddy would want to discuss about the hazardous changes in communities and families. Perhaps the talk goes to the hazardous status of the world, especially the disobedience and lack of discipline of youngsters. You wonder, "Is this the guy I knew? The child who hasn't done his homework? The child who skipped with me at school? The youngster who created our teachers colorless names? Does he not recall what he was like?"

This "childhood amnesia" arises from the idea of your buddy that a parent is a serious job — which means that a parent needs to be serious, severe and somber.

Many parents learn to wear a bucket of mud, ready to hurl them into the future of their children if the youngsters show symptoms of heading in a path that they dislike. In fact, the muck in the bucket represents rage. It is replenished by talking to others about the general bad condition of youngsters.

You have to let up of your control objective in order to prevent parental rage. Instead, you may affect the conduct of youngsters by making them credible as someone who expects the best. This does not imply ignoring undesirable behaviour; but it does not mean attempting to expose the kid to your wrath. If you take the ideas of the community that "children go hell in a handbasket," you are continually afraid of your own children or, even worse, falsely proud of their cleansing.

Happiness is one of the finest things you can do for your children. Remember your own childhood. Have your parents been glad? If so, wasn't this a fantastic power source for you? If not, wasn't that a big cause of trouble?

The way to show your kids that you are glad is not to let their conduct disturb you. Show children that it doesn't imply that you'll create a life unpleasant just because you need parents (after all, they will make errors, act improperly, and so on). Therefore, because they're not responsible adults, they require parents. But they're going to be.

Making the proposed modifications here will entail life changes for most people. Nobody could be joyful and have trust in their kids at all times, save possibly certain saints. We are sending a sign saying, 'Improvement lies in that way.' Don't be in a position that make you fail with imperfection as a parent. Any improvement in your daily enjoyment with your children will compensate you for your efforts.

Monitoring change enables us to change. You can use four or five pages in your own notebook to document achievements in altering your attitude towards your children, fearing their failure to live up to hopeful expectations and communicating these expectations. You don't have to be miserable to properly parent.

Chapter 2

PARENTING IN THE 21ST CENTURY

Parenting in the 21st century may be everyone's most hard and fulfilling profession. Parenting requires us to sacrifice ourselves and participate with children every day. It summons all of our anxieties as we strive to satisfy children's developing and often emotional demands.

On a day-to-day basis, parentage may provide us countless tiny delights, which come only from seeing and experiencing what they need and love us. It may also give the ultimate personal gratification for effectively meeting children's needs and therefore leading another person to adulthood and maturity.

Parenthood is different in a number of ways in the 21st century. Many of these distinctions are related to the structure of today's families and the time and energy available to current parents to fulfill their obligations. These changes are caused by shifting views and choices as to what kinds of partnerships individuals choose to raise children or are obliged to raise their children. The high costs of having children also have a significant impact on the amount of time and energy now available to raise children.

RELATIONAL CONTEXTS FOR RAISING CHILDREN

U.S. Census Bureau data show that 73.5 million children are present in America.

1 In three main categories of relationship and family situations they are raised:

- Families of two parents (married or unmarried)

- Single parent households (formed by choice or through circumstances such as divorce, death, imprisonment and so on) (reated through remarriage or through becoming a reconstituted family without remarriage)

Naturally, these relationship and family kinds have always existed. It is the shifting numbers in each form of family that make parental status so varied today. In 1970, for example, 9% of children lived in single parent families. By 2000, 28% lived in single-parent homes. 2 Moreover, as 50 per cent of marriages terminate in divorce and the majority of divorced parents remarry, more children are raised in mixed-up homes than ever before and often change the makeup and organization of their families.

The married, two-parent setting is the most conventional relationship situation. Many individuals still attempt to raise their children in this way today.

Research shows that bringing up children in the two-parent environment is an excellent aim for spouses and their children if the marriage partnership itself is good. Healthy marital relationships, as well as any other healthy partner arrangement in which children are brought up, are defined by the commitment of both partners to this connection as a lifetime project, to support each other emotionally and to respond to each other's demands for intimacy. These healthy unions are also free of partner or domestic violence, since healthy partners are aware of and employ non-violent ways to resolve the unavoidable conflicts arising from living together and educating children.

The Department of Health and Human Services of the United States examined a wide variety of studies in which they compared the effects of good and dysfunctional marriage partnerships on the healthy. For example, the research indicated that women in healthier marriages were physically and emotionally healthier, were richer and had better relationships with their children. Men from those partnerships lived longer, were also physically and emotionally healthier, richer and sexually more gratifying. The children from strong married unions were also shown to be emotionally and physically healthier, less of a problem with conduct in schools, less of an academic success, less of a risk for alcohol and other drugs or for criminal actions and more of attending college.

These outstanding results confirm the wisdom of those who strive to achieve good marriage connections. They also have consequences for any kind of partnership in which children are reared.

The results demonstrate clearly that children and young people become better in almost every aspect of life when they are brought up by spouses who care for their relationships well. Everyone is entitled to a healthy relationship.

The significance of the quality of interactions between parents and children is what all the other recommendations deal with regard to whether the setting is a two-parent, single-parent or mixed-family environment. And this is applicable to the interactions between straight parents and their estimated 59.5-69.5 million children, as well as the relationships between homosexual and lesbian parents and their estimated 4-14 million children.

ECONOMICS

Not only are direct money expenditures significant for raising children; they are growing. In 1960, the entire cost of raising a kid from birth to age 17 was calculated to be around $129,000, according to statistics by the US Department of Agriculture (USDA). By 2001, the anticipated total expenses had increased to over $197,000.

Seven categories of charges comprise the direct costs on which these USDA estimates were based:

1. Housing — Includes shelter (mortgage, property or rental tax, maintenance and repairs, insurance), utilities (gas, electricity, fuel, telephone and water), home equipment and equipment (mechanical furniture, floor coverings, major electrical supply, minor appliances). Such housing expenditures are underestimated because they do not include main mortgage payments that the USDA deems part of savings.

2. Food — Food and non-alcoholic drinks purchased at grocery shops, convenience stores and specialized stores include purchases of food stamps, restaurant meals and school lunch expenses.

3. Transportation — include net spending on new or used automobiles, financing costs for vehicles, oil and fuel, maintenance and repairs, insurance and public transit.

4. Clothes—Includes children's clothing such as clothing for diapers, shirts, shirts, dresses and suits, footwear, and clothing such as dry cleaning, modification, repair; and storage.

5. Health Care—Includes medical and dental treatments not covered by insurance, non-insurance prescription medicines and medical supplies, as well as premiums for non-employer or other organizational health insurance.

6. Child Care and Education—Includes daycare, daycare, babysitting and elementary and secondary education and provision.

7. Miscellaneous—Consists of personal care products, entertainment and reading materials.

As far as the cost per year of these fundamental expenses is concerned, the current USDA statistics reveal that they fluctuate because of factors such as the age of a kid, the family's total pre-tax income and whether the husband-wife team or one single parent raises the child.

Depending on the age of the kid, the total annual direct monetary expenditure range is between $7040 and $8070 for lower income groups; between $9,840 and $10,900 for medium income households; and between $14, 470 and $15,810 for higher income families.

8 These figures demonstrate that children's spending is usually lower in the younger years, and this is true for income levels.

Additional data from the same USDA research also revealed that these ex-penses differ by the location in which a family lives. Ex-pensions were the highest among city west families, followed by city northeast and city south. Families are the least expensive in the metropolitan Midwest and rural regions.

However, all of these figures underestimate contemporary children's upbringing expenses as they stem from what the dollar could buy in 2001 and inflation has subsequently lowered purchasing power. Since 2001, several costs – such as childcare, housing and transportation – have also grown. These figures on parent expenditures for raising children do not, furthermore, cover parental spending for children above 17 years of age or the cost of college education.

More significantly, these figures do not indicate the indirect cost of raising children by parents in terms of overall costs for raising children. These include the amount of time that parents spend raising children for which they are not compensated, the pay that parents give up when they look after children in place of working and the professional chances that they lose or delay while they spend time on raising children.

Taken as a whole, these direct and indirect expenditures are rather considerable and should be examined carefully before they start working as parents. Furthermore, these financial concerns have a role to play in how parents raise the present generation of children.

These economic realities and considerations are also the reasons why guideline 16, which provides an excellent example of lifelong learning, calls for parents to seek their own financial literacy training, by learning more about saving, investing and making smart consumer decisions. There is much strong evidence that most parents today could take advantage of this sort of instruction. Take into account:

- Only 27 per cent of Fleet Boston's parents polled in 2003 felt adequately versed about home cost management.

- Less than half of those polled believed they were excellent saving and spending models for their children.

- The average credit card debt of the 25- to 35-year-olds, including parents, in 2004 was $5,200, almost double that of 1992.

- More than 60% of households pay their credit cards with the minimal amount, therefore establishing a continuing debt position.

- 79% of high school students never took a personal finance course.

- 94% believe their parents are their major financial teachers.

Moreover, while the average family income grew 5.8 percent between 1990 and 2005, according to the College Board, the expense of sending kids to school increased. Over that period, the overall cost for sending students to public colleges and universities, which is attended by the majority of students, has increased 63%. Private universities and universities have increased their costs by 47%.

Another significant increase in family costs is the retirement cost. With individuals living longer and health care expenses higher, plus inflation and the prospect of lower social security benefits, the retirement expenditures are considerable. These economic realities are more reasons for parents to be as financially informed as possible and for them to take on the role and duty of financial mentors of their children.

The economic reality of modern living is also the major reason why we now have so many parents, especially two-parent homes. One parent, the mother's associate, used to stay at home to look after the children, while the other parent was working to produce revenue to pay for the family. For two-parent households, this probably ideal scenario is no longer the norm. Now most of the two parents work full or part-time to produce the household money they require.

Finally, it is important emphasizing that money plays a big influence in the way parents can be present and nurtured. With abundant financial means, parents are more free to be present to children physically and emotionally. Not having enough money implies spending a lot of time and energy on just being able to live, which undermines parents' physical and emotional accessibility.

It is a disgraceful and frequently terrible fact that millions of children in our nation are nurtured without sufficient resources in homes. In 2006, for example, of the 73 million children aged 18 or less, 13.5 million were living at or below the poverty limit considered at the time by the federal government ($20,000 in a family of four, $16,600 in a family of three, and $13,200 in a family of two). 13 This huge number of children are the most vulnerable to almost all health risks and they are the most likely to be abused and neglected by their parents. As we go on our voyage across the childhood landscape of the 21st century, it makes sense to recognize that millions of American children are being nurtured under situations which are humiliating and abusive.

PARENTING-ON-THE-RUN

Many of the facts of modern family life discussed thus far lead to a scenario that I call "parenting on the ground." This is a scenario in which parents spend a lot of time and energy coordinating and balancing family and work duties that frequently go unheeded and are thus frustrated and tired a lot of time.

Think about a parent or two parents who must wake up early to prepare children for child care or school and prepare for their work. Then they all have to go where they belong most of the day and work long hours. Then parents pick the children up after work, come home to a fast food restaurant or make supper, dine, oversee homework, control TV and computer usage, and maybe prepare for a work meeting in the morning, and so forth. In addition to these obligations, some children have to spend time in the house of other parents during the week or on the weekends and this often happens with divorce agreements and mixed families, and modern family activities are even more pressurised. Then the main home duties of buying, cleaning and repair are on top of all these sorts of activities. It was this "parenting on the go" that started to characterize the majority of family life towards the close of the last century and now is a feature of so many families at the beginning of the present century.

Because of this kind of stressful scenario, excellent health care is extremely vital. Indeed, addressing one's personal health requirements, another problem addressed in the recommendations on successful, modern parenting, is really a must in order to be able to cope with these strains of 'parenting on the ground.'

CHILDHOOD OBESITY AND OTHER EATING DISORDERS

These pressures can easily contribute to what was known at the beginning of the 21st century as the epidemic of juvenile obesity. Health officials highlighted that the rate of obesity among pre-school children between 2 and 5 years of age and teenagers between 12 and 19 has more than quadrupled in the last 3 decades, and has more than tripled in the case of children between 6 and 11 years of age. Thus, roughly 9 million children over the age of six were deemed obese at the start of this century.

Obesity is generally defined by the use of the Center for Disease Control and Prevention (CDC) Body Mass Index (BMI) chart and it is shown when children and youths between the ages of 2 and 18 have a BMI equal or over the 95th percentile of the age and gender chart.

In our culture, where a trim figure is so coveted, social and emotional difficulties as well as physical health problems are the challenges for children and young people accompanied by obesity. Social and mental health problems that are typically the results of obesity include being socially humiliated and marginalised, negatively stereotyped, mocked, harassed, and discriminated against.

The negative implications of obesity for physical health are as severe. Glucose intolerance and insulin resistance, type 2 diabetes, high blood pressure, sleep apnea, menstruation irregularities, poor balance and orthopaedic issues are among them.

Obesity itself is fundamentally a problem of energy imbalance, where the calories consumed are significantly more than the calories used. Put sim-ply, obesity means too much and not enough movement. The increase in childhood obesity presumably results from a complex social and environmental interaction that affects eating and physical activity. Over the decades, these have worked together to produce an unfavorable global environment to preserve a healthy weight. As stated by the Institute of Medicine authorities, this environment is characterized by:

Urban and suburban architecture that prevent walking and other physical activity;

- Pressures to families to decrease their food expenditures and to acquire and prepare time to often consume convenience meals rich in calories and fat;

- Reduced access and cost of fruit, vegetables and other healthy foods in some places;

- Decreased physical exercise options at school and after school, and less walking and biking from and to school;

- Leisure time competition that was formerly played outside on sedentary screen, watching TV or playing video and computer games.

Many of these aspects of contemporary life, especially those related to diet and exercise, are under the control or influence of parents.

These are obviously the same things that influence or decide the ability of a parent to live up to the speed of modern family life. More parents themselves are obese these days than ever, which stress the need not only for our children, but for ourselves, of supporting and creating a healthy lifestyle.

One of the principal forces that contribute to obesity-related psychological issues also contributes to other eating disorders. The emphasis our society places on a trim body specifically influences an increasing number of individuals, including children and young people, to participate in restricted eating, some to death and even hunger. Nervous anorexia and bulimia are the most common.

Anorexia Nervosa is a significant eating disorder that is typically persistent and dangerous to life. It is defined by the refusal to keep a minimum body weight of 15% of a person's normal weight. Other important characteristics include a strong fear of gaining weight, a distorted corporal image and three consecutive menstrual cycles in women. Bulimia is defined by a harmful binge-eating pattern and inadequate weight control behaviour.

These diseases are predisposed by a mix of environmental and biological variables – particularly girls and women. These predisposition variables include a family propensity towards obesity, poor self-esteem, social isolation, perfectionism, compulsion and the existence of specific predisposing neurotransmitters, in addition to the present culture's fixation with thinness.

In the United States, 0.5 to 1 percent of females develop an orexia nervosa. Of this group, 90% are young ladies and teenagers. Males and children as young as 7 were also diagnosed. Bulimia also tends to start in youth or early adulthood and affects women predominantly too. Bulimia is predicted to develop between 2 and 3 percent of young women.

Chapter 3
THE JOB OF PARENTING

As we started looking at the nature of parenting at the start of the 21st century, we have touched on many of the responses that make up this profession. We also saw that parenting is difficult and demanding, especially in view of the settings and situations in which most parents raise children nowadays.

MOTIVATIONS FOR PARENTING

Why would someone choose such a tough and unpaid job?

Well, people do that as long as people live on the globe, and today most individuals on earth continue to search for and undertake such tasks and duties. Of course, our species could not survive without humans being ready and able to take on this duty.

However, it is questionable that drive is the primary motive to become a parent or a mother. In fact, as with other key decisions to shape life, there will probably be numerous causes and some of them may not be accepted consciously.

Here are some of the explanations proposed over the years that might help you to understand your drive to become a parent. See whether in your personal scenario they have meaning for you.

- Parenting is a societal duty. This drive closest to parenthood, to maintain the species, originates from our fellow human beings' feeling of social duty.

- God's parenting. The motivation here is molded by a feeling of religious duty and responsibility.

- Our people's parenting. This is the reason for opting to become a parent because of a perceived duty to continue with one's own ethnic, cultural, religious or racial group.

- Our family's parenting. The goal here is to ensure that the family or family name continues.

- Generativity parenting. This motive implies parenthood is a phase of human growth in which parents fulfill a fundamental human desire to transfer their own experience and knowledge to the next generation.

- Self-fulfillment parenting. The rationale for parenting here is that being a parent further enhances one's potential.

- Parenting for children's affection. This motive comes from a deep and sincere passion for being and directing their growth in the presence of youngsters.

- Male parenting or feminine proof. The force working here is to show that one is a complete man or woman by becoming a parent or a mother.

- Economic kindergarten. The reason is that children are to be expected to be a financial asset for the family or group.

- Parenting in elder years for support. There a person keeps in mind that when he or she is no longer able to do so, his or her offspring will take care of him or herself.

- Parenting to get a wife. This motive comes from the notion that willingness and being able to have children influence or decide whether someone wants to marry you.

PARENTAL FUNCTIONS AND RESPONSIBILITIES

Different incentives to become a parent can influence how much people engage in the daily tasks of raising children. However, these everyday tasks must be completed out so that children can live and thrive.

Many of these activities were addressed as we studied how to be a parent in the 21st century. Now let's put them together more systematically to get an overall respect for and on behalf of their children, what modern parents do for and.

Parenting is the child-raising process and encompasses a wide variety of activities. These actions can be seen as including five connected functions and their duties.

Provision of resources

These duties include supplying a range of resources needed for the maintenance and maintenance of a house and family. These include material resources (housing, clothing, equipment, furnishings, toys, games), nutrition resources (food, beverage), resources of utilities (gas, water, electricity), services (physical, dental and mical services; educational services), community resources (parks, shops, churches), cultural and leisure resources (films, music, art), and communication resources. communication resources (television, computers, telephone, radio, newspapers).

The education, employment and income of parents substantially dissuade them from providing these resources, which has implications on their other tasks. Where the capacity to offer is strong, the chance to cultivate additional functions is increased. There are fewer opportunities if the capacity is constrained.

An essential component of the supply of resources includes parents' consumption priorities. Do you prefer to buy or rent home in a more prestigious and secure neighborhood at the cost of luxury or needs for holiday and clothing? Do they opt to buy an expensive automobile or to personalize a car for their children at the price of educational materials?

Another component of the resource provision is the link between what most parents have to do to produce resources — work outside the house — and what they do at home. Today the problem of combining work and family duties is greater than ever, because the vast majority of parents are employed. Who remains at home when the children are sick? Who's more important career or job? These resource-related issues and challenges are now part of the life of almost all parents.

Care of the Home

These duties include basic maintenance (cleaning, painting, gardening, plumbing), maintenance of clothes (cleaning, washing, ironing, stitching), maintenance of nutrition (shopping, cooking and dishwashing) and automobile maintenance (cleaning, repairing). Care for the house also includes budgeting, administration and money investment. This covers the daily administration of finances, as well as gambling and speculative investments and donations to charity, causes and disaster relief.

Child Protection

Parents are the people who generally defend family property and resources. They also defend the physical, mental, spiritual, ethnic and cultural integrity of the family against dangers from the natural environment and from people, organizations and institutions.

Some of the risks that parents safeguard children from are:

Bodily harm threats. These are dangers to the life of a small kid because the youngster does not comprehend the threat, such holding hands on fires or roadways. It also involves dangers to children of all ages, such as physical abuse and rapes, cigarettes, alcohol and other substances, from other people. And now, as we have previously seen, parents need to be more cautious in protecting children from and obese HIV/AIDS and other predisposing STDs.

Psychological damage threats. The depreciation of the talents, features and looks of a kid by those inside and outside the family is included here.

Peer harm threats. This involves connections with antisocial peers and peer groups (gangs), for which parents also need to be more vigilant these days.

Social damage threats. Discrimination in social institutions, especially school, against children of different genders.

Race, ethnic, cultural and spiritual damage threats. These are to safeguard children from harm accompanying a degradation of ethnic, cultural or religious values and practices.

In one area, harm to children has consequences in others. An newborn with head or brain injuries may become mentally disabled and acquire a limited or delayed range of intellectual skills. A kid who is injured due of a degradation of his or her ethnic or religious group may not be able to disagree with social, political or economic factors and develop a negative sense of self-esteem.

Protective functions are performed through the physical, social and psychological surroundings of a parent to minimize and buffer the contacts with possible damage to children. Kitchen children's proofing, restriction of access to dangerous play spaces, limitation of access to specific individuals and how children are related to potentially harmful persons and institutions all pertain to child protection. This is how parents guide children to grasp the commercial images they are exposed to, frequently violent, through television, movies, the Internet and video games.

Parents differ considerably in the extent and the extent to which they perform these protective tasks. There is a strong need for parents who cannot afford ideal safe living circumstances and who are themselves victims of prejudice. Parents need to be particularly alert in safe buildings where plumbed paint chips are available for children to ingest and drug trafficking takes place outside apartment doors. Parents must work hard to tamper and to safeguard children from these kinds of psychological and bodily dangers if a parent and kid racial, ethnic, or religious group is susceptible to prejudice, discrimination and stereotyping.

In the performance of such protective responsibilities, child abuses are parental breaches or carelessness. Parents who beat and burn children commit physical abuse of children. Sexual abuse or exploitation of minors frequently leads to irreversible psychological trauma, as well as verbal and emotional misrepresentations and repressions. Parents who don't care or know how to watch their children from far away are harming their children.

Guidance for the Child

This function uses physical and psychological approaches to guide every area of the growth of the kid. The motor, sense, perceptual, physical, cognitive, linguistic, social, emotional, moral, spiritual, sexual, cultural, educational and economic development of children are all included.

Physical care refers to tasks such as nursing, washing and clothing, caring for your health needs, medical help, taking care of physicians and dentists and taking care of your rest and sleep.

Psychological care consists in nurturing and accepting children, disciplining children and helping them to learn the social property of behavior, helping children to make them presentable, guiding children towards the proper functioning of women, teaching children about the world, supporting children in formal education and crisis management (i.e., inculcating moral, religious, ethical, and cultural values in children).

The difference between physical and psychological care does not suggest different and independent processes. The way newborns are fed can, for example, substantially affect the child's sense of acceptance. If you feed cheerfully and carefully to the youngster, the child will probably feel more acceptable. If done in fact or automatically, the kid is more likely to feel disenfranchised, even if the physical requirements of the child are satisfied. The more concentrated activities in physical care are also activities through which parents may contribute to meeting the other needs of a child.

Parents vary greatly in the way they care for children physically and psychologically. The parents' temperament, personality, health status, sex and developmental stage, gender and the presence and influence of other family members, socioeconomic resources of the family, external stresses to the family, the whole community and social context, are all contributors to this variation, which involves the temperament of the child, the health status, personality, gender and developmental stage. Regarding enculturation, a number of parents are highly active and very aware of how and what their children are teaching about their own cultural group. Other parents are less conscious and embody their children just by the way they interact to them.

There is also variety in the parts of the kid that parents feel a responsibility to guide. Some parents, for example, may not regard it as their job to guide the religious or spiritual growth of their children. Variability is also caused by ignorance. For instance, a parent may be accountable for assisting a kid with his/her sexual development but may not be able to provide or perform such advice.

In fact, there are many parents who do not know how to lead different parts of the growth of their children. And they don't know how to do it, since nobody has ever been teaching them. The recommendations and tools are offered in this book partly because so many parents are at this disadvantage.

Connection and advocacy

Children, especially young children, need to be represented before different organizations and institutions because they themselves have no status or ability to do so. It is a crucial aspect of parenting the connection and advocacy of children to these groups and persons.

Parents are the link between children and various groups and connect them to their family of origin and the extended family. Parents maintain this role by also linking children to the realms of child care and school, health workers, tradesmen, transit networks and, eventually, the world of employment. Parents can physically attach their children to these individuals, organizations, or systems as is a rather typical occurrence in what we call parenting-on-going when they personally carry them back and forth. Parents also use access to television, telephones and the internet to link their children to the outside world.

This liaison role also involves ensuring that the children are adequately cared for and cared for by health professionals, childcare workers, educators and other individuals responsible for children. Getting children to these locations and people is only half of this essential responsibility of parenting. Parents must speak to and connect with these institutional representatives and guarantee that their children's best interests are maintained.

As with the other four tasks, parents differ a great deal in the ways that they carry out and interact with these obligations. Again, a reluctance to participate might have to do with not being educated on how to participate. For instance, a parent may not be able to engage school officials because the parent simply does not know what the basic criteria for parental participation are.

The capacity to organize and handle all five of these parental responsibilities simultaneously. As predicted, parents are very different in their performance of this broad and potentially overpowering parenting characteristic.

Families are structured in a number of ways in carrying out these five duties. The tasks are divided between two parents in many families, with one parent accountable for one set of functions and the other responsible for a different set or, in other situations, each parent sharing each function or each function's distinct aspects.

There are households in which the parents help others in doing specific duties. Some families have duties other than parents, such as grandparents, older children, families, friends or even the state. And, as we have seen, there are many single parent families where one person carries out all of the five roles, and more and more families reconstructed by divorce or separation, where more than one parent takes on the tasks, and where sharing is a very difficult affair.

Naturally, these are not the only things parents do. Most parents today have to work to perform their resource supply job. Your profession or career not only leads you to encounter people and institutions that influence your parenthood, but also involves you mentally as far as your career ambitions, deceptions and accomplishments are concerned. These personal elements of employment might also influence parenthood by influencing moods and availability.

Parents frequently have friendships, civil and religious affiliations that demand attention and cultivation, besides working interactions. They also have their relationship with each other or with a partner or another, if they are one parent.

And more and more parents have exhausting emotional ties with their aging parents. These personal relationships can have a major impact on how they do their parenting tasks.

Finally, parents establish contacts with themselves. They may be part of a network of family members, friends, members of religion and employees, but they are distinct persons. The creation of their own individuality amid this complex web of relationships might be as difficult as the fulfillment of their many tasks.

Of course, parenting itself is an extremely difficult undertaking and it is entrenched in a number of other relationships and societal pressures. It is a difficult task which requires knowledge and training to be as effective as possible.

It is also an attempt to be educated and influenced by the greatest available research on the best possible means of doing this. Fortunately, there is a lot of sound research available to assist plan a successful voyage.

Chapter 4

PARENTING GUIDELINES

16 suggestions are presented to assist you raise healthy, happy and successful children. These criteria might also serve as benchmarks for assessing your own family status. You may use them to evaluate if you are doing the best for your children and what else you might do.

1. Give children warmth, acceptance and respect

2. Enjoy the development of your children and be alert to special needs.

3. Use fair leadership and firm management

4. Avoid corporal and verbal punishment.

5. Start early in school preparation for children

6. Create a home environment for education

7. Be an active partner in the school of your child

8. Manage the obesity and eating-related problems of your child

9. Teach children about own and other cultures Children

10. Teach children about drug abuse

11. Teach kids about sexuality

12. Teach children to succeed and give financially

13. Manage exposure to your children's media and technology

14. Keep a healthy lifestyle

15. Enhance the relationship you raise your children

16. Set a Good Lifelong Learning Example

Many of the suggestions are based on the results of decades of study in parenting children. Others are the recommendations on modern parenting and difficulties for which considerable study has yet to be carried out on how best to cope with them. However, many intelligent organisations, many experts and I have trusted in their expertise.

Each rule is accompanied by specific examples of the kind of parenting required. There are also extensive descriptions of parental skills and approaches about how best to relate to a guidance and how to utilize skills and approaches. These skills and methods are the ones taught in current parenting skills development programmes.

1.GIVE CHILDREN WARMTH, ACCEPTANCE, AND RESPECT

Children must feel they're loved and wanted. They must feel welcomed and know that their talents, their appearances and their feelings are pleasant and essential. You must be respected. They learn how to respect others, especially their parents. You, the parent, need to regularly show sentiments of respect, gratitude, warmth, happiness and love – if you can, daily.

- Kiss your children, embrace and touch them.

- Use affection words consistently. "I adore you, I love you!"

"You're enjoyable to be there!" "I just love to be with you!"

"Honey, you look lovely."

- Praise good conduct.

"I'm really glad you hampered your clothing!"

- Encourage your children. Your children. "You're able to accomplish it!"

- Send "I" good messages.

"I feel relieved when you tell me where you are and I don't worry."

- Take the time to listen truly.

- Take time for informal conversations about your child's matters.

- Give children options so they feel that in their life they have some authority.

Let other people know how much you adore your child and appreciate it—and make sure your youngster discovers what you say!

RELATED PARENTING SKILLS AND APPROACHES

The way to be effective

This is a systemic way to ensure that your praise not only gives love and gratitude to your children, but also informs them about what you think is an acceptable or proper conduct. When you teach your children what you think is appropriate, you also teach them the values of your family.

Values must be practiced if children are to be real. If you value collaboration and act cooperatively by assisting others or helping others around the house, your kids will perceive your cooperative value as true.

When you praise your children, you enable them to teach the values of their families. The particular actions you commend are behaviors that reflect your ideals. The fact that children are praised when they play or cooperate with one other, when they pick up themselves or when they talk in an honest tone shows that you value collaboration, responsibility and respect for others.

The implementation of the Effective Praising technique needs your children to be excellent. You are then prepared to apply the seven Effective Praising steps:

1. See Your Child

2. Move your child close

3. Smile!

4. Say to your child a lot of kind things

5. Praise the conduct, not the child

6. Be physically affected

7. Immediately move into action

The first three phases relate to the body language utilized for Effective Praising:

1. See Your Child. You must gaze at the youngster before you can praise a child properly. This allows the youngster realize that, in particular, you talk to him or her.

2. Move your child close. This amplifies the potency of louange since it is far more intimate and personal.

3. Smile! Sometimes a grin alone makes someone else feel good enough. Imagine how strong a grin can be when combined with much praise.

Now, what are we saying?

4. Say to your child lots of kind things. The aim is to create a lot of what your child does—to show you the child attentively and say a lot of good things like: "Thank you!" "It's lovely!" "Well done!" "Good thought!"

"I enjoy it when in that voice tone you talk to me!" "That pleases me very much!"

5. Love the conduct, not the child. This is a very crucial step: ensure your conduct is praised and not your youngster. Praise your youngster for what he's doing, not what he's doing. For example, there is a world of difference between saying, "Paul, it's been pleasant helping me to clean the dishes," and adding, "You are a good kid, Paul." The first transmits the news that Paul received praise for his cooperative conduct and washed the dishes. The second sentence is just an opinion or view about Paul as a person and does not provide any information as to what he accomplished.

The remaining two phases are concerned with demonstrating affection and the optimum moment to praise effectively.

6. Be physically affected. A embrace, a kiss or a touch on your shoulder can make your praise really warm and personal for your kid. Don't be frightened of showing your devotion. Get physical when you compliment your children.

7. Immediately Go Into Action. If you realize desired behaviour, it is vital to congratulate your youngster. If you've "taken" your youngster to clear the table, immediately congratulate him. Don't save it later or five minutes later in the day.

So now you've got it: all seven stages plus instructions on how to implement them. Thousands of other parents who have mastered this Effective Praise seven-step technique showed outstanding outcomes. Their children ally themselves again like being treated like this and love being recognized for doing the right thing. Some kids even begin to praise their parents! This is one of the strategies taught in the Confident Parenting program, the "Effektive Black" and the "Los Niños Bien Educados" programs for African and La-Tino American parents. If you utilize these two programmes, or any family or culture that has evolved its own distinctive means of showing gratitude, then these expressions can be used for what you commend.

In many African American families, for example, recognition is conveyed by using phrases such as "On One!" or "Hey, that's too difficult!" or "Go, girl/go, guy!" or "Get on!" Using ethnic or familial expressions gives extra layers to your love and makes everyone appreciate the way the youngster acts.

Approach to encouragement

This method to warmth transmission is seen in parental training programs such as active parenting and systemic training for effective parenting (STEP). It provides not just warmth and acceptance, but also helps youngsters learn from errors without focusing on them. It helps kids learn to trust themselves and their skills. In a spelling test, for example, a youngster missed five of 25 words. Instead of going through the five mistakes, a parent who utilizes and believes in encouragement would point out the proper 20 words. By concentrating on what is positive, the parent gives the kid the impression that all is all right. The youngster knows the five mistakes; it doesn't need to be pointed out. Acceptance of the youngster enables her to feel valuable as a person.

It is especially crucial to learn the approach of encouragement if you are accustomed to discouraging youngsters. You prevent children from having unrealistically high expectations, for example if you want them to do well or every hair on the head, or when you expect their rooms or personal spaces to be "as clean as a pine." You also discourage children if you create contests between siblings or sisters, or if you expect cleanliness in the household from certain children but not from others.

The use of encouragement indicates that the good is emphasized. It includes utilizing sentences that indicate a child's acceptance and words that acknowledge effort and improvement such as: "I appreciate the way you did it."

"I admire your manner of dealing with an issue." "I'm happy you love to study."

"I'm happy that you're happy with it." "It seems like you liked it."

The promotion approach includes communication and confident phrases: "I know you, I'm sure you're going to perform well." "You're going to make it!"

"I trust in your judgment."

"It's a hard one, but I'm confident you're going to figure it out." "You're going to figure things out."

Fostering also involves focussing on the contributions made by children and offering appreciation through comments such as: "Thank you very much."

"It's been thinking of you. ."

"Thank you, I truly appreciate it because it facilitates my work."

"On .. I need your assistance."

To a family group: "I liked it very much today. Thanks."

"You've got ability in. Would you do this for your family?"

A very essential aspect of adopting the encouragement approach is to recognize children's efforts and improvements by communicating, for example, "It appears like you really have worked hard."

"It seems like you've been thinking about it a lot of time." "I see you move along." "I see you move along."

"Look at the advances you made." (Specific, say how.) "In . you improve." "You improve." (Specifically)

"You may not believe your objective has been achieved, but look how far you have come!"

Caution Note. These and the other positive communications you have learned can discourage youngsters from using a 'I told you' or an arrogant attitude. Do not give with one hand and take the other with you. In other words, avoid qualification or moralization.

For example, avoid communication like: "It seems that you've really worked hard – why not always?"

"This is time!"

"If you try, see what you can do?"

Remember, the primary reasons to use the encouragement approach are to believe in your children so that they may believe in themselves, accept them as they are, highlight good features of their conduct, recognize efforts and improvements and express gratitude for the contributions they make.

When you acquire the art of effective praising and encouragement, you develop abilities and concepts that you may work with other adults. Most people love being complimented and encouraged and feel good to those who acknowledge their positive behaviors and efforts. With your wife, other family members, acquaintances, colleagues and employers, you may apply these talents. This allows you to obtain other relationship benefits since you have spent time and effort learning how to apply these talents correctly and often.

2.ENJOY YOUR CHILDREN'S DEVELOPMENT AND BE ALERT TO SPECIAL NEEDS

The growth of children, especially in the early years, is interesting. Day by day, week by week, something new happens: they may move towards noises. You can make push-ups for babies. You can grip and bring something to your mouth. You may speak what you hear — and then and then in an increasing collection of talents and abilities.

Experience these early triumphs. They are the building blocks for thinking, reading, writing and communicating.

- Learn about the various child development regions and stages.

- Read development books for children and visit parenting sites.

- Make regular use of The Discovery Tool during the first five years of your kid's life, a set of questions that show you how your child is growing compared with other children of her or his or her age.

A sample of questionnaires from The Discovery Tool is accessible in the Appendix.

Some children do not grow normally, and it is vital to find out so early. These are children with more requirements than the ordinary child—children with special needs or impairments. In any or all areas of development, their particular requirements can be met. It may be difficult for them to walk, hear, see, learn, talk or communicate with others. Their demands might be moderate or high in these areas.

The sooner they are identified and supported, the greater their chances to complete school, get work and live on their own. Be attentive to the possibility of unique requirements for your child. The Discovery Tool is handy here again. It lets you know whether your child has special needs and where can you turn for support in your neighborhood.

About the tool of discovery and related resource development

Let's spend a little time on The discovery tool, because its usage may be very useful for children's development and for alertness to any issues.

The complete Discovery Tool may be accessible over the Internet 24 hours a day, 7 days a week, at ciccparenting.org. All questions are available. There are numerous questions concerning your child's present behavior and your child's birth and medical history. You complete the questionnaire prepared for children aged between birth and age.

As indicated before, an example of these surveys may be found and used in the Appendix.

The completed questionnaire will allow you to describe the present conduct and skills of your kid in the following six key areas of child development:

1. Engine and physical growth of the body

2. Thinking and learning: cognitive growth

3. Communication: Language development expressive and receptive

4. Senses: Vision, hearing, touch and integration of senses

5. Concerning Self and Other Persons: Emotional and social growth

6. Self-care: everyday skills improvement

The majority of questions in each field relate to the abilities gained by the average kid in that age group up to that point. These are known as "developmental milestones." For instance, in the field of body motion or motor development, the average child may use his or her hands to scoop or punch to pick a tiny object such as a cheerio or raisin at the age of 9 to 12 months. This nice small achievement, a building block in which to learn how to write a pencil, is a milestone in this field.

Such "small" achievements are just as worthy as the first walk or the first word of the child. Knowing that these are milestones will increase your appreciation of the growth of your kid and will be brought to your notice using the Discovery Tool.

The Discovery Tool also warns you that the general development of your child's talents may be delayed. It also allows you know whether some of your child's present actions (or absence of certain behaviors) are in keeping with others or learning more about the world.

When taken online, the Disocovery Tool scores your answers automatically and gives you the resulting sheets you may print. The results highlight any delayed qualifications and probable problems. You must enter the tool yourself, and there are instructions for doing so when you use the example version in the Appendix.

If your kid still has several skills to develop or has many problematic behaviors, you are notified to visit a competent medical expert, such as a developmental assessment or check-up psychologist.

You'll find further information on the development fields covered by The Discovery Tool in Chapter 5, Parenting Children with Special Needs, as well as more detailed information on developmental assessments. You will also be given information on what you can and should do if a kid has specific requirements.

In terms of learning about children aged 5 and above, several publications are important. The American Academy of Pediatrics has also released books, such as Caring for Your School-age Child: 5 to 12 years old, and Care for Your Adolescent: 12-21 years old.

USE FAIR AND FIRM LEADERSHIP

- Recall the rules to children: "Remember, we are putting feet on the floor, not on the table."

- Hold family reunions to establish rules so that everyone can work together to resolve issues and disputes and take decisions.

- Provide specific incentives or rewards for family rules.

- Give clear verbal directions.

- Redirect attention: "How is it possible to play this game rather than to touch these harmful garden tools?"

- Try a "time-out" when all are anxious.

- "I feel frustrated to see my clean kitchen unclean again. I don't want to spend my whole day cleanning it." • Give strong "I" messages:

- Use the approach "First / Then": "First finish your schoolwork and then email your pals."

- Try to find solutions that are pleasant to both you and your children wherever feasible.

- Remove privileges for significant infringements of the rules.

- Try contracting. - Try contracting. You can establish an arrangement to alter your own conduct in return for changing your children.

More family rulers and specialized skills

These examples of fair and strong leadership and the Coin Design of Family Rules are most effective once you have obtained a more complete and thorough assessment of the issues involved. This also applies to the warmth and acceptance examples in the first guideline. This guideline has been used to exemplary effective praise and encouragement and, thereafter, to explain the specifics of their usage, to provide you a general knowledge and the steps to follow in the application of these abilities. Remember that these are skills taught in the context of current parenting programs. All these instances of firm and fair management and the Coin Conception have also been taught in numerous current parenting programs.

Here you will discover more about the relevance of family law, the coin design and the characteristics of two of the aforementioned talents.

The significance of family rules

There are numerous reasons to have and be explicit about family rules. First, family rules assist youngsters to learn which of their behaviours. Indeed, family norms are arguably the most important approach for parents to teach children acceptable behaviour. If parents are explicit about family standards, they know which of their behaviors their parents respect.

Another significant reason for family regulations is that they enable youngsters to know what they anticipate. When kids know what is anticipated, they feel safer. Family norms can therefore offer a sense of stability for youngsters.

A third good factor is the adoption of rules to prevent issues. When children understand and are motivated to obey the rules and perceive that your kid is going to breach a rule, it can avert conflicts and tensions by simply recalling the rule. For example, reminding the kid of the sofa rules ("Remember the rule of the couch? We are sitting on the couch; we are not standing or springing on it") might avert furious struggle or reduce the need to have a greater impact.

Of course, if this sort of preventive reminder is to work, your children must be encouraged to obey the rules. There are numerous ways to inspire children to praise them and to encourage them to obey the rules, or to make sure they realize the reasons for the regulations. The provision of explanations for the norms of the family, which I call "Appeal to their minds and not their hinds," is an approach sometimes neglected, and is extremely useful. In the example above, the reasons why you don't jump on the sofa are because leaping can break down or wear out the sofa, and makes the couch seem worn and ragged. Everybody desires a residence of which they can be proud.

Another reason for family regulations is that they contribute to organizing family life. They assist everybody in the house know what is expected of them and when to do it in some ways. For example, it is simpler to do the tasks that must be done in the morning, when everyone knows the rules for morning time and getting ready for school.

Another essential reason for the norms of the family is that they make sure youngsters are trustworthy and grow up. For example, explaining rules on family property management, like operating a family CD player, not only teaches your children what acceptable and appropriate conduct is regarding this important ownership of the family but also shows their children that you trust them to comply properly with the CD player.

Another example is when you tell your youngster why and how to remove the garbage. Here you let your youngster know that the child is old enough to take up more household care. To assume greater responsibility is an indication that the child grows up and matures.

Another extremely essential reason to have family norms is to promote a sense of family unity, collaboration and pride. Such sentiments assist families to stay together.

Until youngsters are able to comprehend and appreciate the reasons for family regulations and the value of them, they will most likely regularly breach the rules. You should really expect a lot of rules in every child's growth at an early stage. Remember, kids don't come into the world knowing what's wrong and right. How you react when kids don't obey the rules is essential and some good examples have already been offered.

Here are a few more details on two of the above techniques.

The application of mild social disapproval

This is a way to give precise instructions in a strong voice. It's a quick and efficient technique to control the conduct of your child and its use saves everyone involved a lot of wear and tear. It consists of seven essential components, like the art of successful praising, each contributing to the total efficacy of your parenting:

1. See Your Child

2. Move your child close

3. Have Facial Expression Disapproving

4. To issue a letter or command (fewer than three sentences)

5. Keep your voice at a low level

6. Make a disapproval-consistent gesture

7. Immediately move into action

Mild social condemnation must, by its very nature, be applied gently, smoothly and swiftly to be as effective as possible. It aims to rectify behaviors that breach rules before they get out of hand.

Use moderate social criticism to keep things under control immediately after realizing that rule-violating conduct (misbe-have) is going to be initiated. Typically, mistreatment increases in severity, collecting strength and energy as it expands. Early social rejection can save everybody a lot of trouble later.

Here's a case in point: John and Mary, your 3-year-old twins, play peacefully on the floor of the living room with their blocks. You quickly observe that John becomes upset with Mary, since she won't share the blocks. Shortly afterwards, John begins to yell at Mary and picks up all his blocks. Mary doesn't like the attack on John, so she clobbers one of the blocks on him. Now the struggle is on and you have to separate two screaming children. They're all heated and troubled, and when you get the scenario right, chances are you'll be too.

This complete spectacle might however simply be prevented by setting limits with a certain timely, moderate social criticism soon as the pot started boiling.

A father who felt problems once the kids started to struggle with each other and promptly responded to it with moderate social criticism may have saved himself and his kids from much unneeded pain. Walking up to Mary, staring in her eye, pointing a finger, and asking, "Share the blocks with John, please, Mary," surely would have been enough to avert the resulting frenzied scratches.

So be fast with a small social disagreement. If you can smell problems building, answer straight away. It may take some experience to learn to detect danger situations early on, but as a parent you are undoubtedly well-informed in this respect.

Return praise quickly

Now, after you have utilized moderate social criticism, you have only done half the work needed to make this process as efficient as possible. Mild societal condemnation alone teaches just what your youngster doesn't want to do. It solely covers the "no side" of the coin.

A skill such as effective praise is a better instrument to instruct a youngster to be more courteous. It is therefore important for you to follow with a large dosage of praise all the positions of moderate social criticism when your child begins to act properly. This may at first be hard, as most parents are simply not used to louing the chil-dren so soon after they have misbehaved. This, however, is the best approach to teach your youngster healthy behavioral choices. Try your best to follow with praise the disapproval sequence after your youngster begins to act more correctly.

When your children participate in rule-breaking conduct, you have many additional abilities to utilize, including the ability to deal with severe offences. Several have already been proposed, such as "time-out" or privilege removal, or the establishment of unique incentive systems where your children gain advantages only when they earn compliance awards. The specifics of all these abilities here are beyond the scope of this chapter.

To conclude this section, however, we will examine a another parenting technique, which is especially useful for older children and teenagers: contracting.

Chapter 5
POSITIVE PARENTING WITHOUT ANGER

Every parent occasionally gets upset with his or her children.

It is no assistance now that remote schooling or changes in school curricula are available and we are attempting to deal with the restless, bored, screen-addicted children at home. There are numerous pressures: zoom appointments, items we have neglected up to the last time, health and financial concerns. Between that tension, come into our kid who suddenly recalled that she never took her school work today, tease her younger brother, steal the screen time, or is very hostile. And we're snaping.

But as complicated we find the conduct of our child, their behavior doesn't create our anger. When we are in a healthy state, we may occasionally remain patient and empathetic and settle the storm.

But we are prepared to over-react if we are stressed — maybe in the thick of a pandemic! We witness the conduct of our child ("I struck her again!") and make a conclusion ("He'll be a psychopath!") that prompts other inferences ("I have failed as a parent!"). This avalanche of ideas generates an arduous train of feelings — dread, consternation and guilt, in this case. Those sensations we can't bear. The best defense is a good attack, therefore we're angry with our youngster. The entire procedure takes two seconds.

Your child could press your buttons, but it doesn't cause your response. Every problem that makes you feel like being caught has roots in your early years. We know this because at that point we lose our capacity to think rationally and start acting like children, throwing our own tangles.

Don't worry. Don't worry. That's normal. That's normal. We all arrive into parental relationships that are injured in some manner from our children's lives, and all those wounds appear to our children. We may anticipate our children to act in ways that sometimes throw us over the edge. That is why it is our responsibility as the adult to stay away from the edge.

How can we get so angry with our children?

Parents and children can trigger one another as nobody else can. Even as adults, with our own parents, we are often unreasonable. (Who's stronger than your own mother or father to distress you and make you childish?)

Similarly, because our children are our offspring, they push our buttons. Psychologists call this phenomena "ghosts in the nursery," meaning that our children stimulate the strong sentiments of the children we live in, and frequently subconsciously re-enact the past, which is adorned in the depths of our psyches like forgotten hieroglyphics. The anxieties and fury of childhood are potent and even as adults can overwhelm us. It might be quite difficult to set these fantasies to rest.

It helps to know all this if we fight to manage with rage. Just as importantly, because it encourages us to regulate ourselves, we have to be aware that parental anger might hurt young children.

What happens when you scream or hit your child?

Imagine if your spouse or wife loses his anger and shouts at you. Now picture them three times bigger than you, overwhelmed by you. Imagine that you are totally dependent on him for food, housing, security and protection. Imagine that they are your main source of affection and trust and global information, which you have nowhere else to turn. Take whatever sensations you have summoned and multiply them by 1000. That's like what occurs in your child when you're upset about him.

Of course, we all become upset, and occasionally outraged, with our children. The task is to call on our maturity to regulate and therefore limit the detrimental impact of this rage.

Wrath is frightening enough. Calling names or other verbal abuses that the parent disrespectfully talks to the kid will bear a greater personal burden, because the youngster depends on the parent for his own feeling of himself. And children who endure physical violence, including spanking, have demonstrated enduring bad impacts, from lower IQ to stormer relations, to a higher chance of substance misuse, which reaches everywhere in their adult life.

If your young boy doesn't appear to be scared of your rage, it is a sign that he or she has seen too much and established barriers against it – and against you. The unpleasant outcome is a youngster who is less inclined to satisfy you and is more vulnerable to peer groups influences. You have to conduct some repair work. Whether they express it or not — because the sooner we get furious, the more protected they are and so less likely to exhibit it — the more scary our children are our fury.

How can you deal with your own wrath?

Since you are human, sometimes you are in "fight or flight" mode and your child is starting to appear like the enemy. When we're overwhelmed with fury, we're ready to fight physically. Neurotransmitters and hormones flood our systems. You make your muscles tighten, pulse to race, and breath accelerate. It is hard to remain cool at these periods, but we all know that it isn't really what we want to do to cover our children, while it may provide immediate solace.

The most essential thing about rage is NOT to behave in anger. You will feel urgent to act in order to teach a lesson to your youngster. Your fury is talking, though. He believes this to be an emergency. It's almost never, however. You can teach your child afterwards and that will be your lesson. Your child doesn't go anyplace. You know where she lives. You know where she lives.

Now, do not strike, do not swear, do not call your children's names or discipline when you are upset. What about yelling? What about yelling? It's never a tantrum for your children. If you absolutely have to cry, get inside your automobile rolling up the windows and yell where nobody can hear, without using words, since they're angering you. Just yell. Just yell.

Your children are also furious, and thus finding productive methods to cope with your wrath is a dual gift to them: you don't just harm them but provide them a role model. Your child will surely see you upset from time to time and youngsters will learn a lot from how you deal with these circumstances.

Will you educate your child that could be right? That parents also have sobbing? This shout is how grownups are dealing with conflict? If so, they are going to adopt these habits as a sign that they are grown-up.

Or will you model your child that anger is part of a human being, and that it is part of maturity to learn to control anger responsively? This is how. Here's how.

1.   Set limitations AND you become furious.

Often it's because we've not put a boundary to our children, and something's grinding at us. As soon as you feel upset, it's a sign to do something. No, don't shout. Positively intervene to prevent additional conduct that irritates you.

If your annoyance comes from you – say you simply had a rough day, and your enthusiasm is wearing on you – it might help to explain it to your children and urge them to be careful and to keep an eye on your annoying behaviour, for now at least.

If kids do something more and more annoying—playing a game where someone is probably hurt, stopping if you asked them to do something, struggling while on the telephone—it may be necessary to interrupt what they are doing, re-establish your expectation and redirect it so that the situation and your anger are not escalating.

2.   Relax BEFORE you take action.

If you're upset, you need a means to relax. Awareness will always enable you to take advantage of your own self-control and change physiology: Stop, Drop and Breathe. This deep breath is your pause. You have an option. Do you truly want those feelings hijacked?

Remember now, it's not an emergency. Shake your hands out of the stress. Take another ten deep breaths.

You may try to discover a technique to laugh that releases tension and changes mood. Even pushing yourself to grin sends your nervous system a sign that there is no urgency, that it begins to relax you. If you need a noise, sweetie. It might help to release your wrath physically so you can attempt to put some music and dance on it.

If, during school or naping, you can find 15 minutes a day for a practice of attention, you may strengthen your neurological ability so that it will be simpler to calm down at these upsetting occasions. However, even everyday life with kids should offer you lots of opportunity to practice, and if you avoid acting when you're furious, you change your brain to better self-control.

Some individuals still follow the time-consuming suggestion of clobbering a pillow, however it is ideal if you can perform this sort of discharge in private because it may be rather terrifying for your kid to see you clobber. He is well aware that the pillow is a medication for his head and that the image of a mum who strucks insane is sewn into his memory. This is probably an unsuspecting approach anyhow, because research shows that striking something — anything — verifies that this is truly an emergency, and that you should keep "fighting." Thus it may "unload" energy and wear you out, but it won't get at the sentiments that cause anger and can make you angrier.

If you can instead breathe deeply and accept the furious sentiments, you will probably discover that fear, grief, deception are there behind the anger. Feel these sentiments as you notice the sensations they create in your body. Do not strengthen them by "thinking" why you are unhappy; breathe in this tension in your body and watch it transform and diminish. The anger is going to dissolve.

3. Take five.

Recognize that a furious state is an awful starting point for any issue. Instead, give yourself a break and come back when you can settle down. Move physically away from your child so that you're not tempted to reach him and touch him. Just say, as gently as you can, "I'm just too furious to talk about it right now. I'll take a pause and relax."

Exiting doesn't allow your child to win. It convinces them how severe the offense is and demonstrate self-control. Use this time to relax, not to go into another frenzy as to how right you are.

If your child is old enough to leave a minute, you can go to the bathroom, sprinkle water on your face, and breathe. But if you're young enough to feel abandoned when you go, they'll follow you shouting. (This is even going to be done by many adult partners. Just to say.)

If you can't leave your child without getting angry, go to the kitchen sink and run under water your hands. Sit on your child's sofa for a few minutes and breathe deeply and say, like one, a small chant which restores your serenity, "This is not an urgency."

"Children need love most if they're least worth it."

"He's doing it because with his enormous sentiments he needs my support."

"Love just today.

It's okay to recite loudly your mantra. It is good role models for your children to see that your strong emotions are handled appropriately. Don't be shocked if your youngster takes up and starts to utilize your chant when he is upset.

4.   Listen rather than act on your anger.

Like other sensations, anger is as important as our arms and legs. What we have to do with it is what we choose to do. Anger frequently contains a worthwhile lesson, but behaving while we are furious is never productive, save in rare instances that need self-defence, since we make decisions that we will never make from a reasonable state. The productive method to deal with rage is to reduce our expression and diagnostically utilize it when you calm down: what's so wrong in your life that we're furious and what must we do to alter the situation?

Sometimes the answer is obviously connected to our parenting: before things go out of hand, we have to enforce regulations or start bedtime half an hour earlier, or restore the bond with our child to stop it treating us unpleasant. We are sometimes shocked that our fury is really towards our spouse, who is not our entire partner or even our employer. Sometimes the explanation is that we are dealing with anger, we don't understand that it spreading to our children and must seek treatment via therapy or a support group of parents.

5.   Recall that "speaking" your anger might reinforce and intensify it to another person.

Despite the widespread belief that we need to "express" our anger to prevent it from eating out of us, the idea of releasing "fury" to someone else is nothing beneficial. Research reveals that expressing anger while our rage makes us really angrier. That in turn hurts and frightens the other person, making them more furious. Not surprisingly, this increases the gap in the relationship rather than addressing anything.

Moreover, showing rage is not genuinely sincere. Anger is an assault on the other person, since within you feel so unhappy. True honesty is the hurt or anxiety that leads to rage - which you might do with a spouse. But with your child, your duty is to control your emotions and not inflict them on your child.

The answer is always first to calm down. Then examine what the underlying "message" is before you decide what to say and do.

6. WAIT before to discipline.

Make it NEVER an angry point to act. Nothing says that you must issue fly edicts. Simply say something like: "After we spoke about how striking hurts you can't believe you struck your brother. I have to think about it, and this afternoon we will talk about it. I want you to be on your best behavior till then."

Take 10 minutes for yourself to calm down. Don't pick up the issue – that type of stewing will only make you more upset. Use the aforementioned strategies instead to calm down. But if you took 10 minutes and still don't feel calmly enough for a productive relationship, don't hesitate to postpone the debate: "I want to think about what just occurred, and we'll speak about it later. Meanwhile, I have to have dinner and please do your homework."

Sit down with your youngster after supper and, if necessary, impose tough limitations. But you may listen more to his perspective and respond to his conduct with fair, enforceable and courteous limitations.

7. Avoid physical strength, whatsoever.

85 percent of young people claim their parents have been slapped or smacked (Journal of Psychopathology, 2007). Yet, studies after studies have shown that punching and every other physical punishment has a lifetime detrimental influence on the development of children. The American Academy of Pediatrics strongly advises its rejection.

Personally, I wonder whether the epidemic of anxiety and sadness among adults in our culture is partly driven by the consequences of so many of us who grew up with parents who mistreated us. Many parents minimize their physical aggression, because they recognize the emotional anguish. However, suppressing childhood grief just makes us more prone to hurt our own children.

Splitting may briefly make you feel better because it sends your fury away, but it is harmful for your child and eventually sabotages all the wonderful things that you accomplish as a parent. Screwing and even slapping has a way to escalate. There is even some evidence that spanking is dependent on the parent, because it offers you a means to release that disorder and feel better. However, there are better methods for you not to damage your child, to feel better.

Do everything you need to do, including to leave the room. If you can't control yourself and end up turning to physical strength, apologize to your child, explain him it's never OK to hit and get assistance.

8.   Avoid menaces.

While you are furious, threats will always be ridiculous. Since threats only work if you are prepared to comply, they weaken your authority and make it less likely that your children will next obey the rules. Instead, inform your youngster that you need to choose a suitable answer to this violation of the rules. The anticipation will be worse than hearing a succession of threats that they know you will not push through.

9.   Monitor your choice of tone and phrase.

Research reveals that the calmer we talk, the calmer we feel and the calmer people react to us. Similarly, we and our listeners are angered by using swear words or other highly charged phrases, and the issue has escalated. We have the capacity to soothe or disturb ourselves and the person with whom we talk through our own voice and word choices. (Remember, the role model is you.)

10. Still furious?

Don't get angry. Don't get angry. Once you have listened to it and made suitable modifications, let it go. Recall that if that doesn't work, rage is always a defense. It protects us from the vulnerability.

Look at the hurt or fear of rage to get rid of it. Perhaps the tangles of your kid frighten you, or your daughter is so preoccupied about her pals that she dislikes the family that hurts you. Once you acknowledge and allow yourself to feel the underlying feelings, your anger will disappear. And you may act more constructively with your child to resolve what appeared to be an overwhelming situation.

11. Make a list of appropriate techniques of dealing with rage.

Sometimes, when things are quiet at home, discuss acceptable methods to deal with anger with your children. Is it ever all right to strike anybody? Is it all right to chuck stuff? Is it all right to yell? Recall that since you are the role model, your child's rules apply to you as well.

Then write the appropriate methods to deal with rage and put it on your fridge to read periodically by everybody in the household. Let your children watch you check it when you become upset.

"What you want to tell the other person without criticizing them."

"Set your angst on music and dance. "If you'd want to strike, tap your hands around your own body and grip yourself."

12. Choose your fighting.

Your youngster uses important relationship capital with every unpleasant contact. Concentrate on what counts, such as how your child respects other people. The bigger scheme of things might make you crazy with his jacket, but it's not worth pushing your financial account into the red. Remember, the more your child's bond is good and linked, the more likely it is to follow your instructions.

13. Consider you are part of the problem.

When you are open to emotional growth, your child will always show you where you have to work. It's impossible to be a calm parent if you're not, since everything will prompt you to do the worst. We have the power to soothe or aggravate the situation in every encounter with our child. Your child may behave to make you worse, but you are not a helpless victim.

Take responsibility first for managing your own emotions. Your child may not become a small Angel overnight, but you will be astonished when you learn to keep cool in the face of her wrath, how far less furious you are.

14. Continue to search for effective disciplinary approaches that promote better bsehaviour.

There are far more effective forms of discipline than cold, and research in fact suggests that angry discipline establishes a loop that promotes misconduct.

Some parents are astonished to discover that families seldom discipline children, even with penalties or periods and parental screams are uncommon. There are of course limitations and behavioural standards, but this is reinforced by the parent-child connections and by assisting children with the needs and disorders that drive their "bad" behaviour. The research shows that these families generate children who are emotionally smarter and can thus regulate their conduct more effectively.

15. If you fight with your anger often, get advice.

There is no shame in asking for assistance. It is a shame that you disregard your responsibilities as a parent by physically or psychologically hurting your child.

How to Get Kids To Listen Without Yelling

Parents claim they do this mostly because they want to listen to their children, but they have zero cooperation. If promises, pleadings and threats are no longer working, screaming might be the only choice. Especially when the time is limited, behaviors are out of boundaries and major power struggles erupt and shouting becomes the means to persuade children to listen.

The trouble is that shouting at youngsters doesn't actually help them focus on what they desire.

Katie Hurley, parenting expert, explains why:

A natural child defensive technique is to shout out. It's a really loaded input. Children may shout back or even laugh in answer, but they don't internalize the message. Having frequent yells can cause signs of anxiousness in youngsters and lead to a difficult to stop bad cycle of communication.

Here are some pro-active methods to try to decrease shouts and encourage children to listen and cooperate:

Set limitations early

Sometimes we fear possible tears, conflicts or protests with limitations. So in the first place, we avoid establishing the restriction. This is the problem? This strategy of avoidance leads to irritation and animosity on our side until the last minute. Then we shout, our kid shouts, shouts, or disconnects.

Setting a limit earlier implies that the problem is removed long before it increases and causes screams.

Keep your limitations and remember to confirm your feelings

Sometimes setting limitations means that kids feel upset. However, maintaining limitations encourages youngsters to trust our direction. Although we cannot possess or alter the sentiments of our children, we can attempt to accept, sympathize and guide them with confidence.

It is really important to confirm your sentiments and then believe that your child can experience and go forward. Here's a chat I had lately with my four year old:

Me: "Can you put the place mats on the table, please?"

Four years of age (with inventive excuses): "Oh, but hurt my legs! And I play with my mobile phone!"

Me: "Oh no, your legs hurt? me (showing curiosity) What's happening to them?"

Four years old (being honest!): "Ugh, I don't feel like Mama's table arrangement. This is really dull!"

me: "Uhm.uhm..you don't feel like that. You don't feel like it. This is uninteresting. It is dull. I get it. I understand. And it's time for dinner. So what is your plan to accomplish your job?"

"I don't wannnna, four years old. I don't... I don't mom."

Me: "This is a dull work. You don't want to. You don't want to do it. Can you do a fun job?"

4 years old (understanding my request didn't change): "Can my princess playmobil do it? With my aid, you know?"

"Yes!" me: "yes!"

See more about limitation and frustration assistance.

Fit expectations

Young kids touch everything, preschoolers question why about 300 times a day, school pupils frequently don't care when we believe it is time to do it. If the expectations correspond (at this time!) to the skills of our children, the better they can do with our demands and no longer need to shout.

Connect before requesting

Children are much more likely to comply with request, even better at or below eye level, when it is done face to face. This is a very secure and linked approach of requesting a request. What's more, you demonstrate a fantastic manner that your child may connect with classmates, siblings, teachers and friends when you talk gently.

Of course, being near also implies you are lowering your voice, which is quite essential.

TRU parenting Andy Smithson says that loudness is a great difference. "The louder we are, the less... Logically, we believe that a louder speech enters the ears and boosts hearing. The problem is that when we raise our voices, the free-flow switch for our children flies and puts them on the defense immediately."

Motivating youngsters to take part in jobs, to finish their schoolwork, to play well with a sibling may all feel like an endless struggle. Children develop and learn therefore they need good direction every day. Although it may at first seem like more work, it's less stressful to be courteous with your demands and it also inspires more collaboration.

Positive Parenting Techniques

Each parent will undoubtedly reach a break point at some time in his/her parenthood, where we raise a white flag and declare to ourselves, 'there must be a better way. There has to be something to alter."

It may be the middle of the evening with your three-year-old, who has you in a zombie state, tangles on the supermarket shopping aisle, or a reverse conversation that flashes your nose.

Your break point may be because the argument in your house increases, your children don't listen or you are constantly caught between being furious and hopeless

Do not quit up if you believe you're out of choice and at the crossroads of "this doesn't work."

At the end of the tunnel there is a light, and some methods may be put in your back pocket to assist you discover greater serenity in parental care that you haven't felt in a while.

With a couple of them, sometimes as simple as you, you won't believe they work like magic until you witness it with your own two weeks, changes, fresh perspectives and some familiar methods, you will feel more secure and ready to take up whatever parental task is ahead and shout.

What's Yelling Doing To A Child With Parents

No parent likes to scream at their children, I know.

I get it. I get it. I know how awful it feels to shout at your kids.

I don't want to raise my voice in order to attract my kid's attention, stop them from fighting with each other or deal more with disrespectful behaviour.

It's not a smart approach, I realize, and it never improves a problem.

(It doesn't work!)

It also makes me feel terrible about my parenting skills.

I can tell you this during all my research and training how to stop screaming and examine the true reasons that parents shout too much.

Parents shout because they are driven to the verge of fury by stress, internal triggering or other conditions, and believe that they have no more effective means to utilize.

For parents who shout too much, shouting might be a default strategy

In Daniel Goleman's book Emotional Intelligence, he quotes the study of Dolf Zillmann, a psychologist at the University of Alabama who showed that the physiological consequences of rage can persist for days and rage feeds on fury. Repeated aggravations - "a succession of provocations" — can significantly raise fury such that a person responds to an outpost key or a dropped spoon with a third or fourth rage trigger at level 10.

Recent study shows that screaming makes kids more aggressive, physically and verbally.

Unfortunately, if fury becomes "normal" in your family, current research suggest screaming has the same adverse consequences on a youngster.

In the research of children with yellings, increased anxiety, depressive symptoms, tension, behavioral difficulties and other emotional illnesses are long lasting effects.

Not what any parents want for their child, but what kind of parenting methods can we employ every day to prevent our temperament from flooding with those we most love?

Use positive parenting methods rather than shouting

Reactive strategies do not work when you try to use positive childhood

Say, for instance, you're at the shop and your kid finds an item they really desire.

They must have a fresh figure for action, or so they believe.

Well, action figures are not included in your buying list nor in your budget and that's not its birthday either.

Suddenly, fireworks start and your youngster causes a scene since they don't come. He doesn't go down without a battle!

How are you reacting?

Throw the toy into your cart to keep it happy and calm and finish the fit.

Threaten that he will have an impact or lose a privilege if his behavior does not cease,

Make him angry and photograph the situation he made,

Reactive methods are not strategies at all, short-sighted answers, which create long-term difficulties, do not cure behavior, and worse, harm your child's relationship.

Let's consider each of these reactive techniques and what each is about.

1. Enter and get the game

When you surrender and purchase what you want your child, and then fit when you say no, the long-term effect is that you have indicated you can control your child easily.

When a youngster learns that you're a push-over, they keep pushing the envelope over and over again to obtain what they want since they've learnt that they can.

If a youngster is told "No" and then no follow-up, as painful as it might be, this is the area where in children the sentiments of entitlement, greed and power come from.

Are you ready every time you go to the shop for recurrent tantrums?

Taking in may be the fastest and easiest method to stop a tangle, especially if you're in public, but it's tougher to take in and implant in your road the sentiments of entitlement and not appreciation for things he earns or gives him.

2. Threats and punishment

Trust me, I have been down this route and it's hard to get back from it and requires a lot of consciousness to change and constantly.

Because empty threats have a long-term damaging impact.

Think about it. Think about it.

Will you truly be successful when you return home in 20, 45 or 60 minutes?

Will your youngster comprehend their punishment after so long?

After all, children are highly short-sighted and as they seek instant satisfaction from a toy, snack, treatment, affection, etc., so rapid action is necessary as regards behavior-related consequences –> the result is lost on them.

Will it truly affect their conduct next time?

I know I have threatened emptiness in the hope that my kids are going to behave in the shop or while we are in public, but I have seen here why this strategy never

(never) works:

I can't follow a consequence straight away, so why should my child first trust the threat?

Any effect I give my child when we get home is unconnected to what is happening in the shop. In the shop they desired a toy, for instance, but at home they lose privileges for TV or device which have nothing to do with each other. Another connection lost again.

3.   Lose it in the Aisles store and yell unleash at your baby.

It may be because you have said "no" to your child 5 times, or you've had your hands full of two other kids. It may be because last night you did not sleep well and you were weary or just ashamed that your child was acting like such.

You don't want to shout, but you want to halt the behavior right away. Plus, no, no, no, no.

That's when you're raising your voice and shouting.

"We don't receive the toy. How many times must I say?!?"

Yelling probably stops the tangling for a time, but you've undoubtedly attracted other shoppers' or people's attention in public and you are shameful now, embarrassed and guilty.

Does shouting stop a behavior again?

Perhaps not.

How can you parent without yelling?

Take a deep breath first and realize, as a parent, that you have utilized one or all of these three techniques.

This parenting trip is like running an ultra-marathon every week. It's long, it's difficult and the path will always be obstacles and unexpected hurdles. There are also these beautiful sweet-spots, which make you feel that you are at the top of the world if you discover them and are in a nice rhythm.

All the reactive tactics I mentioned above share one thing: they're REACTIVE. This means that you don't stop looking at your child or the circumstance with a certain lens; you just attempt to get rid of the issue as fast as you can.

Stop the tantrum. Stop the tantrum.

Stop complaining. Stop whining.

Stop fighting. Stop fighting.

Stop weeping. Stop sobbing.

Get children to sleep. Get children to sleep.

See what I mean? See what I mean?

It's all about how fast you can reach the finish line.

Discipline tactics such as time-outs, shouting and disclosing irrelevant implications are all linked to these common rationals:

You don't want to see why your child mistakes or acts because you want to stop your conduct as fast as possible.

You react by shouting, since it was trained from past shouting events to feel good - studies demonstrate that your release from shouting is akin to a drug euphoria and addictive qualities. Crazy, okay?

You react to problems by shouting since you don't have to utilize other tools.

Responding parentage is demanding and drains you more than proactive parenting physically and emotionally.

Since we ultimately decide how we feel, it is vital for parents to know their sentiments. To adjust the reaction of the body to stimuli and notify our brains of the flashing red light we must halt. Otherwise we will lead our anger and react in a way that is different from the parent we wish to be.

This also involves being keyed into the sentiments of our children.

Set aside 10 minutes a day to charge

I recently heard a webcast about stress with guest Dr. Chatterjee from his new book, The Stress Solution.

We live in stressful times as a busy mother, company owner, wife, housewife and many more "work" titles we have called these days.

Certainly, many things happen to us every time we insert something new in our calendars, but that insatiable urge to stay busy drives our culture. And you cannot not be drawn down by it.

What truly opened the eye was what Dr. Chatterjee called microstress doses that begin the minute you wake up and pile up faster than you would expect.

What happens if you get a micro-dose of stress over and again?

Simple.

You reach a point of rupture and then you REACT.

You snap, shout, shoot chocolate in your mouth, and are less gentle and caring for yourself and your surroundings.

Let me give you an example of what he is talking about in microstresses.

You set your alarm at 6:03am and it push you out of deep slumber when it goes off. This is your first stress micro-dose.

You click the snooze, cuddle in the warm blankets again and the alarm starts again. Now you're running behind the stress micro-dose.

You hurry downstairs, leave the dogs away, start preparing breakfast, prepare sandwiches and try not to forget... All stress micro-doses.

Your dog's breakfast gets thrown up. (It's just me? Between my three dogs, I swear that occurs to me once a week. Stress micro-dose.

Sally says that as you push the children out of the door she forgot her book and doesn't know where it stands, tears begin.... Yep, another stress micro-dose.

I'm not going to put you through such a day, but you get a sense of where this is leading.

It's rather simple to receive stress hits quite fast, isn't it?

Each of us is continuously assaulted with various scenarios that feed us with a small amount of stress, and we have 20 under our belt before long, and the next person to ask for a snack may "stop."

What, therefore, does Dr. Chatterjee suggest to do with these stress microdoses?

There are a few things he proposes, so you have to understand what works best for you, but his testing shows that all you have to do is plan to press the reset for 5 or 10 minutes in the morning.

You may go to a gym, sit outdoors, write a diary, have a cup of tea, meditate, read 3 pages of your book or listen to music, and spend 5 to 10 minutes watching or in nature.

(The study claims that if you look at fractals that are seen exclusively in nature, plants, trees, etc, you may feel calmer instantly. How awesome is it?!)

Stay off your phone, all right?

Why is this essential in the morning?

You don't want to wait until you have "de-stressed" the children. After all, you have already developed a healthy supply of microstresses and you will be more prone to snap, scold, weep or be harsh, and those around you will be harder by 14.00 if you don't pre-emptively do something about them.

That's exactly why clicking the re-set button in the morning following the assault of AM rush microdoses will offer you a new start.

We all don't want to be the greatest parent we can be?

Well, we can accomplish that only when we take care of ourselves and make sure that this micro-dose of stress doesn't hinder our children's listening, empathy and relationship.

2. 10 solo connection minutes per day

I try to fill their attention bucket 10 minutes a day with each of my children.

Not only does it let me know what is happening with them, but the time we both look forward to and the more connected I'm, the less my kid is wrong, and I don't cry out as a reactionary answer.

Ten minutes a day of undisturbed playing is crucial for connection and relationships. It can be easy to create a fort, play basketball, color, read a book or dance in the kitchen.

It is likely that if you fill in their buckets before time, when you need to perform a job, call or be busy with another activity, kids will be better behaved and will respect your time.

3. Empathize before your answer

Instead of shouting at your youngster, try to connect.

Comfort them with their physical contact by stroking their shoulders softly or by drawing them into a hug and showing them their sentiments.

"I know that toy friend you really wanted. Something you can't have is difficult to want. I know just how you feel."

Let your child know that you acknowledge their sentiments, that they are legitimate and essential but that you can also be part of his team and that you can unstoppable what he is doing.

This may not totally end your tantrum, but it teaches your youngster that you do not mean no, still worry about him and understand his great feelings.

3. Get to the root of conduct

There is usually something that motivates the misconduct of a youngster.

The behavior itself is merely the sign of something going on in your child.

You could be over the tangle or whin, but what causes your youngster to act like that?

It's because he doesn't have the talent to communicate his emotions, he tries to gain your attention, he feels detached, he has a power play at work or perhaps he hasn't got the capacity to regulate his sentiments.

There is always a cause for conduct, and it is the task of a parent to play a detective and to figure out what is behind the bad and/or disruptive behavior.

When you discover the core source of the problem, you may become a more proactive parent and prevent future outbursts.

5. Consistency is the key to discipline without shouting

Children are thriving on routine - they enjoy its constancy because it makes them feel comfortable, lets them feel in control of their environment and self, and the same goes for rules and consequences.

When you have established limitations in your home – expectations, house regulations and routines – and if something goes off the line or a border is crossed, then everyone knows precisely what to anticipate.

To be a proactive parent, please ensure you properly express your rules so that children are aware of the consequences if those rules are broken.

And if they are broken - you need to respond quickly so that children can witness you follow through.

For example, if your child is to make his bed, put his clothes away and clean his teeth and hair alone in the morning, but they don't, what is the consequence of failures? Do they have to clean another section of the home or sweep across the dining room and complete their morning work?

Routine cards work wonderfully well to create a routine, including tasks, and remind children of what comes next and help them become autonomous.

For parents, it's a win-win! No fuss, no recalls, a clear list of tasks they all need to accomplish on their own.

6. The effects must be linked to the behavior

In order to carry out the consequences, parents must be explicit in their expectations and guarantee that the repercussions are connected to the misconduct.

If an impact like losing technological rights results from striking his sister, the relationship between the two cannot be understood by a youngster.

A better option may be that the youngster should sit down and not play with his sister or other friends since he hit somebody.

Children must be able to comprehend in advance the repercussions if they make an incorrect choice, and a parent must not cry.

9 Essential Tips Positive Parenting

Decades of research have proven that the use of positive discipline has beneficial results for the conduct of the kid and emotional maturity.

In contrast, harsh, punishing early childhood parenting likely to lead to greater behavioral issues. Cold, uninvolved and inattentive parents bring up children with a deteriorated self-regulation which further exacerbates children's behavior problems.

THILL RELATIONSHIP PARENT-CHILD

A positive mom doesn't have to penalize her child for correcting bad behaviour. No more screaming, battle for dominance or animosity. This changes parent-child interactions and enhances their bond.

In addition, mutual respect and open communication enhance the bond between parent and kid.

Best of SELF and MENTAL WELL-BEING.

Children brought up with pleasant childhood have better self-esteem. They think they can accomplish things just like most other children.

These youngsters are more resilient, too. They are ready to rebound from adversity.

Children who are self-confident have less family conflicts and greater links with their loving parents. They tend to improve mental wellness.

GREAT PERFORMANCE SCHOOL

Children with positive parents have higher academic achievement. A better parent-child connection has also been very much linked to the success of the school.

Better Societal Competition

Positive parent children have higher ability to solve social problems and social autonomy. They are more adapted and have a good self-conception.

More select and more strest parenting

Not just children gain from excellent parenting. Researchers discovered that parents who practice positive parents also acquire confidence and self-esteem in their parenthood. They are less stressful since youngsters have autonomy and are well-behaved.

1.   FOCUS ON THE THE BEHAVIORS

There is always a reason why youngsters misbehave, even though the parents can find it stupid.

It's reasonable for the youngster, which is why they do so.

If parents are able to deal with the problem directly, even if the kid does not get precisely what they desire, they still feel they recognize their needs. Emotional support from the family is frequently more essential than fulfilling the real desire.

A recognized youngster can go on without misbehavior. You may still be grumbling, but you don't have to act to hear it.

Ask them questions and get to the heart of the issue. The use of attentive listening and knowledge of the cause behind the problematic behaviors may also initially aid parents to prevent them.

For instance, a youngster struck her sibling. The explanation might be that when her small brother grabbed her toy, she was frustrated. So it's not possible to educate the younger child first to request permission before stealing someone else's things. Doing so also teaches kids excellent ways.

There are two probable explanations if your child seems to never hear you.

One reason you might not have realistic expectations. Review what your child is asked to do or not to do. Is that a request or a command? Has it a valid reason?

A youngster is simpler to accept a decent explanation, particularly one that is relevant for his well-being, than to follow an instruction mindlessly.

The absence of intimate parent-child interaction is another reason for disobedience, which provides the basis for child growth, brain development and future achievement.

2. Be Child and First

Be kind to your child to demonstrate how you are kind to others and polite.

By imitating others, children learn, and you are their primary role model.

When a parent shouts, humiliates or calls a name for a child, when they become irritated, the youngster learns to do the same thing.

The opposite is also true. When a parent remains polite and respectful while agitated, the child learns to deal with calm and respect challenges.

Being nice also helps a youngster settle down, be open to thought and collaborate more.

It is not the same to be kind as to give in.

Many parents erroneously equate that they are positive and nice to permissive.

That's just not true.

You should still establish limits, but you should apply them in a compassionate and strong way at the same time. You can say to a youngster, for example, firmly and politely that she can't have what she wants. You don't have to shout, use a medium tone or speak sternly. A rough voice transmits wrath whereas a strong voice transmits authority.

You don't have to mean business. A company and a quiet NO is as good as a loud and harsh NO, if not better.

You may set limits and implement consequences firmly so that your youngster understands what to anticipate and on which to base future decisions.

This practice enables youngsters to develop their cognitive thinking, an essential skill for their future success.

3. DISCIPLINE GENTLE

Positive Discipline According to Jane Nelsen, the first three years of punitive punishment are four Rs who do not benefit the kid, resentment, rebellion, revenge and retreat.

Often, artificial negative effects cannot halt harmful conduct or teach beneficial behaviours.

If parents shout or chastise, a vicious cycle of compulsion is created. Coercive cycle was shown to be linked to behavioral difficulties and behavioral abnormalities, such as child opposition disorder.

A pleasant, non-poisonous reaction is considerably more successful in calming and encouraging an over-stimulated youngster to acquire a new habit.

In recent years, time-outs have been extensively criticized. This is because most parents don't utilize it properly.

Children's timeouts are not supposed to be punishment, yet most parents sadly utilize it this way. They isolate and limit the movement of the kid and add a supplementary punishment by chastising or lecturing the child.

In the original timeout concept, the kid is simply removed from the over-stimulating environment which generates or worsens misconduct and then placed in a non-reinforcing area to relax and to feel comfortable.

Some parenting gurus have thus developed time in to replace time out. Time-in is in fact a notion comparable to the correct usage of time-out that psychologists have proved to work with decades of research.

The only way to halt undesired conduct is not to use time outs. Positive A-Z discipline: 1001 Everyday problem solutions, including from Nelsen, are complete with useful advise, answers and tips on successful discipline.

However, all 1001 answers are hard to remember, or always have a handy book when you need it. It is therefore vital to be innovative and adaptable when it comes to discipline.

Recall that a positive approach to parenting concentrates on teaching the right conduct rather than punishing the undesirable.

4.   Be clear and be aware.

Decide and explain clearly the consequences of breaches of limitations before enforcement. Parents must also be consistent and follow them through

If a parent is not consistent, misunderstanding will arise.

The youngster might continue to try or challenge the limitations to discover what else can happen.

Do not say anything to follow by means unless you mean it.

Do not threaten emptyly to cancele the ball game if your youngster does not do so unless you are prepared to do so.

5. BEHAVIOR-APPRIATE AND BRIAN-DEVELOPMENT

Sometimes, what we believe is wrong is age-appropriate behavior.

Tantrums in kids, for example, are extremely natural. These young children have great feelings but can't express them in words. You don't have the capacity to manage yourself since the brain component isn't formed yet. Our youngster needs our assistance in learning how to control.

Brain development stages have a role in selecting a healthy parenting style. Children and pre-school children (even 3 years old) may not grasp the implications. For them, then, redirection should be utilized instead of reasoning or delivering penalties.

5. EARLY START

Positive childbirth begins with the parent becoming a positive example for the kid and obtaining understanding of child development. So even when your child is just a newborn child, it may start.

Young children learn through looking at their elders and how they behave in various situations. Attending to the questions of your child and reacting favorably may make a major difference in the lives of your child.

Happy children are not born, they are fostered.

6. YOURSELF TIME-OUT TO CHILL OUT

Yeah, that right you heard.

You need to take a break when needed.

Inevitably, parents sometimes feel just weary and angry at the rebellious conduct of children.

But this is the real moment-as-I-say-AND-as-I-do. If you can calm down and talk respectfully and firmly, your child learns to deal with grace with wrath and disappointment.

If things doesn't work in the manner of your child, you want it to be self-controlled and courteous. Don't expect your child to accomplish something if you can't do it yourself.

When you feel like you're going to lose it, tell your youngster you need a time on your own because you're disturbed. Give a time period when you're going to come back and cool off in another room.

Not only does walking away halt the power battles, it also provides you time to relax. Remember your disciplinary aim, which is to educate you not to win in a quarrel.

Take several long, thoughtful breaths to cleanse your thoughts.

You have more time and space to think about solutions to cope with the problem.

You will feel rejuvenated and ready to take up your parental tasks again when you return.

Meditation is another wonderful method to enhance your self-regulation. Regular meditation helps to alleviate stress in such difficult times and improves attentive parenthood.

7.   Make it a learning option.

Each misbehaved event may be converted into a useful lesson in problem resolution if youngsters are old enough to reason (above three years old).

What is the lesson that a toy breaks? It indicates that the youngster can no longer play with it. This is a natural result.

If the youngster did not like the toy, he would have given it to a friend or given it to other kids. Help them find alternate means to express their anger, such as hitting a pillow, when they break a toy out of frustration. Learn how to think about different approaches to address a problem rather than simply act.

Teach them vocabulary, instead of misbehaving, to express their feelings ("I am furious because..."). Help youngsters strengthen their abilities in communicating. Promoting language development will dramatically reduce temper tangles and misconduct.

8.   Be a patient and spare no time.

Positive parentage and positive punishment will not result in behavioral transformations that parents seek quickly.

Positive parenting doesn't mean quick results. It is about teaching that parents desire to emulate their children over time.

Be patient and do not give in to the pressure from other parents who prefer parenting based on fear.

You may have to provide a lot of explanation at the beginning every day. The fact that children require repeats to learn might take longer to observe significant changes than traditional punishment. It may be weeks or even months before your child gets it.

But when it happens, it's highly worthwhile and the rewards endure a lifetime.

10 positive parenting techniques for disciplining your child

Positive parenting sounds at first look like parenting without repercussions for poor behaviour. Unlike many others, good parenting means that you don't react with "I love you" if your 3-year-old strikes you.

Positive parenthood does not mean that our children be kind when they do not deserve it. It is a parental philosophy and strategic technique based on the concept that the most essential thing about our connection with our children is to enable them to develop self-discipline.

To be clear, good parenting is not permissive parenting, which has a high reactivity and low demand. The focus on discipline is positive, and the purpose is to create a child who follows the rules and respects others, not out of fear, but because it is the right thing to do.

Here are several strategies to assist your child acquire discipline and to be a great parent:

1.   Set limits

Limitations in our interaction with our children are essential for a good parenting. Borders have and enforce enables us to stay patient and calm because we feel respected and because our relationship requirements are satisfied.

One simple method to recognize whether you need a new border is to become frustrated, impatient or furious over a repeated behaviour.

Are you afraid to eat because your child is trying to sit on your lap and you can't eat? If so, set a rule that everyone sits for meals in their own chair. After supper, you may cuddle.

Do you feel bitter because every morning your kid wants you to play dolls first while your eyes are still not open?

Set the rule that you can sit and sip coffee for 10 minutes before you can play. Your child's going to complain? Probably. But kids will also start to realize that you also need it.

You will be a better parent if you meet your own wants, and your child will witness a fantastic example of how to argue in a relationship for your own needs.

2. Establish a relationship to co-operation

Remember you have a replacement teacher as a child? Have anybody listened to them? Perhaps not. To listen to them, children must sense a connection to an adult. That's excellent - you don't want your child to hear a random stranger telling them to do anything.

It also implies, though, that your child will listen to you if they feel connected with you. This is the problem of penalty. It puts you at odds with your child, decreases your connection and reduces your child's chances to perform what you ask.

If your youngster has a hard patch with behavior, attempt to connect in a little more one at a time. This does not have to be a lengthy period, but it has to be regular and concentrated. Even 15 minutes a day of your child's free telephone time can strengthen your relationship more than before.

3. Be strong, yet love

There's so much great parenting in the tone. You may be strict and maintain high expectations of your children, while you are kind.

Decide what rules are essential to you, express them clearly to your child and comply with them. To be a positive parent is not to let your child go around you. It means attempting to have a calm, caring tone when your youngster requires memories of the rules.

4. Avoid being shamed

"You're 6, don't act like a kid!"

"They're filthy your room, go clean it up."

"Why can't you listen at any time? It's not that difficult!"

You spoke those words? You said the words? All of these statements have a disgraceful impact that makes youngsters feel awful about themselves. This naturally has a bad influence on the self-esteem of a kid, but it also does not work since it supports the identification of a child as someone who has a specific conduct.

If your child is continually instructed to act as a baby, he or she will internalize this and behave even more in this way. If you call someone a bully, they'll think and act similarly of themselves. Try commenting on the conduct of your child, letting them know when it is wrong, without causing any emotions of shame.

5. Try out the natural effects

Crimination against your child makes you the adversary and may frequently be unclear if the punishment is unconnected to the crime. Instead of punishment, strive to reveal the natural repercussions of your actions.

If you ask your boy to put his rain boots on and they refuse, for example, the natural result is their feet get wet outside. They are far more likely to agree next time it's time to get boots than when they say "no!" to their rain boots.

6. Use logical implications

Although natural consequences are great since they don't set you against your kid, it doesn't always have a handy, short-term effect.

For example, your child might need to leave all of its Legos every day so that you don't tread on them (pain!).

The inevitable consequences, if they are not put off every day, would be for some Legos to be misplaced. It could take weeks or months and may not be able to take your feet.

Try to conceive of a relevant outcome in such a circumstance and do it without resentment. The result may be that if you walk on a Lego, you will place it in your child's Lego bin instead of back in your garage.

7. Use positive strengthening

Did your youngster recall putting all their shoes away? When she was dissatisfied with her assignment, did they aid their sister? Let them know you've noticed!

It's simple to criticize on bad conduct, but just smile when your child accomplishes something nice. Make sure that you pay more attention to positive than poor behaviour.

This doesn't imply that you need a sophisticated compensation mechanism - just tell them what you have seen. Tell something like, "I saw that you all put your shoes away. That demonstrates real responsibility!" Or, Or, "I've seen you helping your sister. You truly care about others."

This type of praise not only helps your child keep a good self-identity that she will want to live up to.

8. Respect for the model

Children mimic what we do. What we do. If we wish to respect people, we must respect them. We must respect them.

If you want your youngster to say "please," please tell them to say "please."

If you want them to wait for you, instead of interrupting you, before they ask them to do anything, wait until they get to the stop.

If you want their siblings to be friendly and nice, be kind and compassionate to them.

In our busy, harried lives, it is difficult to practice, yet children absorb all around them and this surely includes how we deal with them.

9. Fight for empathy

It might frequently appear as if our children are doing wrong to make our life worse. Why couldn't they just obey the park regulations so that everyone may have a great time?

However, there is always a cause for misbehavior, whether it's as basic as a starving child or weary youngster, or more sophisticated as school problems.

If you can grasp the cause of the misconduct, it's so much simpler to develop empathy and answer with love for your child. If you can't figure out why, simply know there is one. Your child loves you above all else and wants to please you, so if they behave, there's a reason.

10. Use time-in rather than time-out

The aim of positive parentship is to establish and sustain your bond with your kid, while at the same time creating a person who does good worldwide.

Time out conveys the message that we can't deal with the conduct of our child, we don't want to see a loud, furious, and chaotic portion of it. It drives you apart.

Time-in or time with your child draws you closer together. It acknowledges that all children deserve to experience their parents' love and acceptance, regardless of what behavior that day looks like.

Time-in isn't necessarily a nice thing. Not all hugs and rainbows are painted together.

It may appear like your youngster is sobbing or throwing a tangle at your side because you keep the line on a frontier. It may seem that you explain the safety regulations that you have and why you had to leave the park early.

Time in doesn't mean everyone is always smiling and cheerful, but it does mean that everyone feels loved, that your youngster gets a message that you always have something there to manage.

Chapter 6

POSITIVE DISCIPLINE

For the same fundamental principle, there are numerous alternative phrasing. Positive discipline is often referred to as positive parenting or even compassionate leadership. Positive parenthood is to recognize your kid as a unique person, to guide you through your lives without harming your originality, while helping to build a moral compass as they grow. There may be a period when children were supposed to be seen and not heard, but the time has elapsed and this is no longer the case.

You recognize your child as a unique person with a good attitude. The first guideline for positive parenting is that you must trust that your child wishes to communicate openly with you and only support it. You listen to your kid and talk to your child about what is occurring so that they learn to self-regulate their behaviour. Threats of confrontation and discipline only go so far unless you have an emotional connection with your child.

The keys to good parenthood:

The first thing you need to know about healthy parental relationships is you need to know clearly what your child wants and what you anticipate. There are keys to effective parenting that open the door to a better road for communication with your child, enabling them to go above your expectations. There are dos and don't, yet these keys and methods are within your reach in this book. Through these

gentle guiding approaches, you may raise a happy, healthy and disciplined kid that will not negatively influence your child's uniqueness or self-esteem.

To be firm and consistent: It is vital that you remain strong and consistent with your child because, without sending it a confusing message, you can set clear limitations and restrictions with your child. Mixed signals will promote misconduct and shatter the faith of your youngster in what you tell them.

Discrepancies Opportunity: In order to practice positive parenting effectively, you must see a dispute as a chance to connect with your kid. Your youngster will grow up to gain negotiating abilities, thinking and even problem-solving skills. Each dispute is a chance for your child to grow as a person, and you can ensure your child grows mature and self independent with gentle direction and positive parenthood.

Making your inquiries: As a parent, you have the right to ask your child about some topics, such as correct conduct. However, you take more honey flies than vinegar and it's no different to raise a child. You must know how to ask your child to do something, and build the right thinking abilities and problem solving skills with positive parenting. They will then come to regard your proposal as reasonable. A child has a better chance of acting if he feels that he is right than if he just follows him because you have instructed him to do this as his parent. If your youngster does not believe your requests, they will be misbehaved.

Please take your time and be patient:

You need to acquire patience with raising your child, and with good parenting there is no exception. You have to be patient with your child and expect nothing to happen overnight. You will have the keys to gentle advice, seven methods for successful parenthood and ensure you remain patient while learning these new ways to talk to your child.

Sometimes it is tough and stressful to communicate, but as a parent, you need to be able to control your feelings so you don't lock your communication door. Don't shout, don't become too upset and never let your own emotions get your best. "Because I have said so," is never a suitable answer and you must be able to treat your kid as a single, rational person to see them grow up to yourself.

Strategy No. 1 Allowing minor misconduct

The first thing you need to know is that every child will go through a phase or time of misbehaviour. This won't be totally gone. Your youngster will sometimes not behave properly. Nobody is flawless and your child cannot be pushed to an unattainable standard, or they cannot find a value in standardizing their feelings that they will never be able to reach. Bear in mind always that your youngster wants to behave. You want to be a nice kid, and you want to be proud. If you believe that you can never do it, or that you will always be let down, then, like everyone else, you will end up giving up. This is why you must always accept little misconduct without a harsh reaction.

Ignore knowing what:

You must know what constitutes 'small' misconduct. Sometimes this conduct may be ignored, but only if it is not hazardous for your child. For instance, if you have a kid and they toss food on the floor, it might be disregarded. You may disregard this if you raise a preteen and slam the door. Do not react. Do not respond. If you reply, you educate your child that this is the way you can react.

If you respond to these little misconduct breakouts, your child may begin to combine them with how you react, get under your skin, and listen to them. You have to respond instead to positive behaviour. Wait for your youngster to relax and try to open communication doors. Don't pay attention to your child because of their misconduct. Positive parenting reactions are possible without entering this loop, which you will read about below.

Positive reactions of parenting:

Silence is valuable due to the least misconduct (s). There is no need to even acknowledge it. Do not pay attention to your child at all, but sometimes you can't stay silent when your youngster keeps acting in what seems to be a recurring pattern. You can remember that this conduct does not get you what you want and that communication is an alternative.

A youngster will feel flattered emotionally like a grownup, and the difference is that they don't know how to manage it most of the time. Many times you may overlook the wrongdoings and wait till your child calms down emotionally so that they can reason things in their brains so that they can tackle the problem a bit more maturely from your example. However, there are some phrases you may use to assist your youngster get a bit easier.

A few sentences:

Here are a few sentences you may use to make sure that the negative conduct doesn't get your children anywhere. Remember they should calm down, but when they are ready, you may talk to them. You must realize that you are ready to discuss when you act appropriately. This will make them feel more comfortable since they want to talk.

Smoothly find a method to remind your youngster that the outcomes they are searching for are only positive. Each youngster reacts differently to different phrases. If you discover a sentence that works, then try using it a bit more. Just remember not to put your child down never and don't talk until you are calm, regardless of what you answer. Otherwise, you're going to engage in negative behavior.

"When you're calmer, I'll talk to you." "I expect you better."

"We're not going to discuss until you're more logical."

"It's all right. I'm going to wait till you have your emotions under control."

Misbehavior Prevention Strategy #2

You now know how to deal with misconduct when it arises and even know what misconduct is safe to allow and what has to be dealt with. However, you can generally also avoid misconduct. No need to wait till it happens. Take an active part with gentle guidance in your child's behaviour. Always be careful with your child, make sure you learn its triggers. No boy wants to be a terrible boy. Children are not as stable or emotionally sound as adults are and even an adult has a trigger.

Triggers Identify:

Are they starving? Are they weary over?

Has your child been bullied? Have they had a horrible day?

Has anybody said anything hurtful? Have they a lot of homework?

Are they stressed absout anything?

You already know when you are able to recognize some of these triggers that your child is more likely to meltdown, which will promote poor conduct. You can support your child even if they experience these triggers. You may even plan on avoiding certain triggers in advance, especially when you have a young child. For example, if you deal with an infant, you can make sure that it is not due of starvation because you can make sure that they feed on a somewhat normal schedule.

However, it can be a little tougher to accomplish with a teenager. This does not mean, however, that it is impossible. You may still make sure that supper is right and that you've always had something to eat in the house for breakfast and lunch. If they are weary, make sure you can sleep for as long as you can. If worried, make sure you have space for an open discourse at home. Make sure you can talk about what stresses you and make sure you know that you can come to you to discuss any problems. This can help reduce the meltdowns produced by these triggers.

Help Phrases Afterwards:

If you know that your child acts on triggers but there is no method or now it is too late to prevent them beforehand, then there are some sentences that you may use to assist reason your child. This is simpler to accomplish with pre-teens or older youngsters. Just remind you that you misdirect your anger and exacerbation, bearing in mind that your child really wants to behave.

"You have to relax. You're not that furious." "You respond only poorly (fill in the blank)."

"Afterwards, you will feel better (fill in the white with food, sleep, etc.)." "I can say you're stressed, but you're better than that." "It's all right to feel stressed, but it's preferable to deal."

"You can talk to me about it if you have an issue."

These words will tell your child carefully that you know they are grumbling or misbehaving, but you know that they can be better and expect it from them. If your child feels that he or she can fulfill your expectations, then he or she will try. If people feel that you are just punishing them for misconduct, they see no need to improve. Your youngster has to be guided to recognize their own triggers, which can avoid future misbehavior. Eventually you will begin to understand your own triggers and strive to calm down. This generally comes with age and you can't expect them to immediately recognize these triggers.

Strategy #3 Quality spending time

When your child feels alone in the world, it will always go through moments, and not every youngster has an easy time for friends. They need to know even among friends that someone at home loves them, cares about them and wants to connect with them. This is the parent's responsibility, not just to be a guide but also to be a buddy when you can. This is not always feasible, but your child has a healthy and joyful connection.

Once in a while your child is significant and it will assist you to modify your behaviour. You don't want to smother your child as it grows older, but it is simpler for your child to have it once a day while it is small. However, you may want to offer your child a bit more room for originality and freedom as it develops. Children are looking for attention and you provide them the good attention they need when you spend a good time with them. Even if you simply have to spend 20 to 30 minutes a day with your child, this is vital for you.

Some ways of doing this:

There are various methods to have a good time with your kids, and if you do it on a weekly basis, you may attempt to do anything like night or night. Recall that film night must be more than a movie. It is vital for you to engage face to face. Take them to the food store, take them with you to buy for clothing, go with your child for a short stroll to get into a healthy habit and give them time to chat to you. Even making a cup of tea and sitting down in the morning to enjoy it can make a difference.

Ideas Weekly:

Movie Night: It's simple to choose a movie you want to see when you're attempting to find anything with your youngster. Don't bring them to the theatre. Not most of the time, at least. You don't want to sit in a gloomy area forbidden to chat.

Some of the plan should be ready to go, to begin a conversation and to talk about something for that week. This makes your youngster feel a bit closer to you.

Family Game Night is wonderful if you are a single parent or even a large family. Family Game Night is great. You can always play games, and from board games to card games all the way to electronic games. When you're having fun, you pay positive attention to your child, which strengthens positive behavior. You are also starting a fun conversation with your child so that they can perceive you as a friend and not simply a strict parent. This helps your youngster to perceive you more than just a figure of authority in his or her life they cannot relate to.

Poetry Share: Actually it doesn't have to be poetry, but you'll discover something that you can share during the week. You can make anything, a picture, a poetry, a short tale, or just a night sharing where you are telling wild stories that came to you that week. You can even do things, but the key part is the dialog that you create while providing your child a positive attention, which they may expect throughout the week.

Classes: You may always take a class with your child. This can be a painting lesson, a poetry class, a sculpture class, or whatever your child's passion. If you are a more active family, even you can play paintballs, but having something set for each week keeps you engaged in the family while associating your spare time with you as enjoyable and something you want to do. The most essential thing to remember is that you should never force it to be something your youngster doesn't care. It will then create a negative connection if you do, and your baby acts before or during the event to try to escape or indicate indifference.

Daily ideas: Things:

Family Dinners: Lunch is a requirement, and there is no reason to travel to various rooms and have a meal. You may take time to have a meal, speak about the food, and talk about your days. Your youngster should be able to look forward to dinner with the family. Do not use dinner to talk about matters or dinner to compel your youngster to talk. Just try to have an open conversation and encourage it, and this may become a good moment to support you on your road to happy parenthood.

Daily Walk: If you want to establish good behaviors in your child, take time to walk, even for a few blocks to 1 miles. Jogging and running may also assist, but walking might make your kid do without them feel as if they are being forced into something. Fresh air might also assist your youngster reduce some of the tension. You will ultimately combine this practice with being able to chat to you or alleviate your tension in a healthy way.

Buying trips: from supermarket purchasing to clothing shopping. You may not shopping every day, but generally you have to run a merchandise or two. Take with you your youngster, but make sure they're not forced to feel. Whether you don't have an order to run, ask your youngster if they want to go somewhere. You could wish to go to the library, the park, a video game shop, or search for clothing. When you inquire what they want to do, you give your child something that they have wanted and remind them that you can be a good part of their lives.

Time of conversation: It may truly be that simple. You have nothing to do. You have nothing to do. If your youngster enjoys hot chocolate, coffee or tea, be prepared and speak for 10 to 15 minutes. This will offer you time to go with you or give you the chance to chat about anything that bodies you. Don't dominate the chat and attempt to keep your baby talking about a topic they want to talk to.

Strategy #4 Laboratory praises

It is generally recognized that when a conduct earns attention, your kid will prefer to repeat this behavior. This is why you should focus exclusively on the behavior you wish to carry on. What most people don't know is that if you penalize poor conduct too severely, it is even more likely to be repeated since it received a certain amount of attention. On the other side, if you name your action compliments that you want your baby to repeat, the behavior will probably happen again more often. Lob your child not only indiscriminately. You have to make sure you only praise your child for something you want to do again.

Empty praises hazards:

There are numerous risks to empty loudspeakers, but the most important one is that you overestimate the meaning of your child. If you tell your child frequently that they do all right, then they don't feel it matters anything. A youngster ought to work on what they do. Not only do they expect everything they do to be successful. Some sentences are just nonsensical.

Another risk of empty louanges is that you may make your youngster feel good about yourself, depending on this louange. A healthy youngster need not thank you for what they feel they can perform appropriately or well. A youngster should have confidence and know that they do not have to be perfect, but that they can perfect what they do.

A youngster should not rely on your assessment, praise and approval. You have to approve what you do yourself. You may even do it someplace your youngster does not want to stay. If you regularly praise children for their actions, such as painting, they will want to continue painting as long as they receive that love. As soon as you stop praising them as much as you had, even if they had a skill in the area, they will drop interest.

You might even lower your child's performance since you are always monitoring their development. An empty commendation makes people feel good, but if they find a fault with their work, they will just get upset, instead of attempting to figure out what may be wrong with it, because you told them that it was fine. This doesn't assist your youngster develop moderately healthy self-criticism. It is what will enhance your youngster.

Examples of empty praise:

When you look at these accolades, you will see that nothing of them is particular or marked. You tell your youngster something that is meaningless. If you say your child is doing a good job, they should know what makes them do a good job. If you just support them by telling them they're doing wonderful, there need to be a reason. Empty compliments won't provide your youngster the advice they need to improve.

"Good job." Good job.

"You do excellent." "It is perfect." It's perfect. "Great work."

Your praises labeling:

If you name your loves, you may educate your child that they do something good without attempting to convince them that it is wonderful.

This will show them that while they have space to develop, they can accomplish things well. You also confirm positive conduct by complimenting your youngster. Subconsciously, a kid remembers this and tries to replicate the act that caused it to be praised.

You also don't have to only congratulate a youngster for activities. You can explicitly commend them for their actions in a circumstance. For example, if your child deals with stressful situations maturely, tell them that you admire how they handle the problem or that during disagreement, they maintain their voice calm. This reaffirms the action and encourages them to repeat it later.

Examples of labeled praise:

Here are a couple of identified praises from which you may utilize and develop, but never just use a generic praise from this list. Customize it to be correct and explicitly describe your child's conduct that you want to repeat or continue. Each of the following compliments is particular, so that your kid can immediately determine what he or she did.

"You control your fury effectively." "You do well." "This test you study hard, and it shows."

"I admire your personal bedtime going so nicely."

"I am proud of your efforts." "I am proud of you."

"You have very neatly sorted out your own difficulty." "Lately your endurance is amazing."

"I honestly think all your hard work pays off." "Your hard ethic shines truly in your school assignment."

Strategy #5 Establishment and adherence to family rules

Another essential positive parenting approach is to have clear and explicit family regulations. You must make the rules, but you must also keep to them. Show your youngster the guidelines for making a strong, happy family unit. There is the 3 R's approach. These are rules, reasons and outcomes. You'll use this approach to define your child's household rules.

Three R's:

The first R is for rules, and it's a particular instruction for your youngster. Make sure it is as easy and as understandable as possible. Make sure you choose a word your youngster can comprehend. For example, when you go to the shop with your child, make sure they understand the behavior you want from them. Say something like: "I want you to stay by my side, and ensure that without permission you do not climb, shout or take anything." All of these are basic phrases your youngster is able to grasp and your rule is quite precise. If a youngster knows exactly what is expected of them, then the rule will be followed more likely.

The following R is for reasons and you should not just wait for your youngster because you are an adult to listen to you. This will not enhance their understanding or judgment. You are supposed to guide your child and to do so they must trust that you have their best interests at heart, or else they often regard it as lunacy. Give a reason, for example, if you don't want your youngster to borrow anything from you. Say something like, "No, because you don't know how to use my curling iron correctly yet, you can't borrow it." If you don't find that you are merely exercising your power because you are the parent, your child will listen to you far more often.

Your last R is the outcome. The results refer to what happens if the rule you have established is violated. This is the punishment that comes, and it is vital to educate your child that it has a consequence or reaction in life when you do anything. There will always be a time when even a decent youngster doesn't make the correct decision and he needs to learn the consequences of his behavior. Warning your kid about a consequence will assist prevent them from making a mistaken choice. If your child did not complete his meal, for example, you would warn them they would not receive dessert. Your kid can then decide whether or not they wish to finish their dish on the basis of whether they are prepared to accept the consequences.

Set them ahead of time:

If you set a rule too late, your child will not be able to assess the rule and listen to it in a fair way. It will probably make things much worse. Never unilaterally create rules in a heated environment. If you need to make more rules, come back and then lay down the rules for your child in a way they can readily comprehend.

Planning is necessary if family norms are to be established and observed. It is therefore necessary to lay out the regulations in advance. If you attend an event with your child where a swimming pool is going to be held, let them know whether they can swim. Let them know what requirements to fulfill for swimming. For example, if you initially have to meet someone, inform them. Tell them whether they need to complete their supper first. Don't wait for your youngster to know.

Strategy #6 Key to redirection

As a parent, you have the right to advise your child not to do anything or simply to say no. However, it is sometimes better to refocus the situation than to just say nothing to your youngster. If a kid continually hears the words 'do not' or 'no,' then it is more probable that the child will begin to tune this out. It's much simpler to turn the child from a misbehavior so that they will listen when you tell them not to do or to stop doing anything. It's the same line of thinking about why you should ignore small misconduct. You can't get to a youngster continuously and expect them to continue responding to you.

Positive behavior replacement:

As a parent, you have the capacity to replace negative conduct with positive behaviour. Often, it's better not to remark on the misbehavior or to attract your attention to it, and youngsters continuously look for attention. You're at a party, for example, and your kid begins to misbehavior and starts telling one visitor something rough.

You see that your child is starting to be harsh, and you have the chance to halt it before it escalates. You won't merely say that your youngster is quiet or not impolite. You may instead divert your youngster by providing it a job. Call your baby and ask if they want a drink. Ask them whether they'll grab anything for you from the vehicle, or introduce your youngster to someone else. Get them away from the negative conduct and redirect it to a positive behavior that your child wants to repeat.

Feedback subsequently:

When you offer feedback later on what was happening, don't give the negative input. Again, never strengthen the negative. Strengthen the good of the day instead. This is the same as labeling your praises, and this approach you may combine with to ensure that appropriate conduct is repeated. Tell your youngster how helpful it was if you sent them to the car. Tell them that you liked how they could walk away from a terrible circumstance, etc. Just remember to focus on the good and don't give too much love. Just enough incentive is okay.

Strategy #7 Set Leniency routines

Positive parenting requires a little regularity, but you cannot be so rigorous that mercy as a parent is not allowed. If your child sees you as a jail guard rather as someone who cares about them, they won't listen. If you open a discussion, you will reply better. Children can thrive on a routine, since it lets them feel safe in a setting.

Defining routines clearly:

You don't want an unstated routine, otherwise your youngster won't see a problem breaking it. You need to be clear that if you want your child to react to a routine you want to maintain. There are times in the day that are difficult for your child but if they have a clear pattern that they can rest on for comfort, then it will be simpler for them to have difficult periods and to complete the day without worry. It would also enable you to connect and share something with your youngster.

For instance, if your child has to wake up at some time, tell them when to get up and when to go to bed. This is common for most schoolchildren. If you want your kid to make a bed, however, tell them they have to make their bed before breakfast and so your kid understands exactly what is expected. Tell them whether they're supposed to come home directly after school. Don't just assume that your child is going to be able to say what your child is going to do with good conduct without guidance. This might lead to bad conduct due to misunderstanding.

The Exceptions Dialogue:

When you deal with a routine, there must be some leniency. From time to time, routines will fail and your child shouldn't feel as if she has to break them if she wants to do something different. Open a discussion on an exception and make it obvious that you are prepared to make exceptions sometimes. If your child wants to see a new film, but it's after bedtime, then your youngster should feel free to speak to you. It doesn't imply that as a parent you are obliged to offer them that lenience, but when you feel it won't damage your child, you have to say 'yes.'

Do not commit mindlessly to a routine just because it's usually done that that. If they can provide you strong grounds for allowing you to view the film, then accept it. But if your child shouldn't really go out for whatever reason that night, like the next day is an essential test, then explain your child why you're saying no. You can speak about a compromise, even then, like taking them that weekend to see it. This helps to prevent a collapse and teaches your youngster that exceptions to the norm exist.

Chapter 7
COMMUNICATING EFFECTIVELY

It can be challenging, but learning to communicate well is vital for a connected family when two people with diverse histories and views are together. As stated before, you each learned how to communicate throughout your childhood. How your parents communicate with one other and set an example of what communication should be. If you have developed negative communication capabilities, it may be a challenge to break out of ancient habits, but we are able to alter if we have learnt anything so far in this book.

The reality is that many of us have learned to give only conditional love and we express this vocally and nonverbally in our communication. We frequently adopt an attitude "I will scratch your back if you scratch mine."

Our own behaviour generally depends on the behaviour, but we may choose a higher course.

We may choose to love even if we don't feel loved.

If others, we may choose to be warm

They're chilly. We may choose to stay calm

Anger face and compassion in reaction to misery.

Effective communication is more than just information exchange. It helps us to better understand our partners and children. It helps us to do this

Connect, solve problems, and transmit emotions. Understanding the emotion underlying information exchange truly is what successful communication really is about. To hear the meaning behind the words is to do with our partners (and others). This leads us to a greater knowledge of the people with whom we share our lives and to better connections in general.

We all need to feel understood and heard, yet many of us aren't adept at communicating what we truly want to say. We may adopt an off-tone in a time of anger, or attempt to conceal our feelings, leading to a lack of communication that makes our loved ones confused and unpleasant. Others still want their wants solely met and do not want to reciprocate, while others instantly get protective and wall off by mentioning particular topics or emotions. These are obstacles that we have to break for our families' sake. It is time to learn better communication habits so that you can create long-lasting relationships.

Are any of these bad indicators of communication true for either of you?

- You disregard emotions. "That's not a huge deal! You overreact!"
- You clamour when there are strong emotions. "I'm all right. I don't want to speak about it, I don't want to talk about it."
- During the conflict, you cry or say harmful things.
- You bottle all your emotions and ideas and then erupt all at once.

- You are over-generalizing. "You're always leaving on the floor your filthy clothing."

- "You're never going to take me out anyplace."

- "You always forget this."

- Your partner is to fault.

- You disparage your partner or put it down.

How many of them who ring true were shown in your home when you were a child? The patterns of communication we have learned in childhood may be redirected with attention. You can learn to communicate

In a way that develops your connection effectively and. It is thus important to set some basic guidelines for communication in your household.

Examples:

- When we're furious, we're not going to debate things; we're not going to bed angry.

- We're going to utilise "I" statements and not blame. We're going to search for win-win solutions.

- "I" will help you get through before "you"

In all your connections, learning how to substitute "you" statements with "I" statements will be helpful. "I" statements are confident, but not aggressive—a it's way to communicate what you need without assaulting your loved one. The manner in which you start a debate frequently affects how the discussion goes, so try to begin with a good note and express your feelings without blameing the other. "You make me angry when you're not coming home on time," for example, isn't a smart way to begin a productive chat. Just like children, our defences kick up when we feel threatened, and we are no longer open to what the other person says. Try instead, "When youbegin late, I feel concerned, and I'm becoming overwhelmed." Typically, beginning a discussion with "I feel when" helps your partner to be more open to whatever you have to say.

A win is a good place to begin

Seek win-win solutions to problems. This is another ability to relate to your parent-child connection. Win-win wants to be cooperative and not competitive. "Win-win is a framework of mind and of heart that seeks continuous mutual benefit throughout every contact," says Stephen R. Covey, author of The 7 Habitc of the

Highly EFFEGTIVE People. It implies seeking a solution that addresses everyone's concerns. In person to do this, everyone must talk in

Depth of its requirements and desires the way both people may meet these needs and brainstorms around a problem.

While this is an easy procedure, it is not always easy.

Many debates include attempting to persuade everyone else why he or she is correct. In person to create a win-win solution, everyone has to be open to the wishes of the heart of the other.

The five-step win-win method is as follows:

1. **Separate the person from the issue.** You may not enjoy the discipline of your partner, but you love your partner. This may seem very evident when no conflict is there, but when there is conflict and both sides are engaged in a tug of war, it becomes rather easy to allow the person get your negative feelings about the situation. Just as we withdraw from a power struggle with our child by looking beyond the behaviour of way and how this person is driven to do so, we must learn to look behind the problems with our partners and look behind them to understand the beliefs and emotions that fuel the conflict.

2. **Evaluation of beliefs, emotions and concerns.** Remember, every person has their own unique storey that has shaped their present beliefs. These different beliefs may create difficulties, especially in parenting, but you will understand the heart behind the point of view and the narrative behind the stance through respectful discourse and empathy. By really attempting to understand the point of view of the other rather than just trying to go around, you open up new options.

3. **Options for exploring, inventing, and rethinking.** Stay honest and open to your partner's suggestions in this brainstorming phase. At the same time, don't be hesitant to say that you don't get a certain concept.

4. **Settle on a solution that both of you feel good.** If you have problems, try to address major concerns. Janet and Dan are, for example, in conflict over whether or not to spoil their children. The main worry of Janet is the detrimental impact on child development. Dan's main goal is to be lenient and not disciplinary. The pair settle for a punishment plan, which does not include spanking but makes sure their child does not deal with misconduct. Both major concerns were addressed.

5. **Give a fair opportunity to the solution.** Test it for a few weeks when a solution

is achieved. If a person thinks that the solution does not work effectively and is dissatisfied, go back to step 2.

To take it for granted

It is always better to inquire than to assume. Assumptions about the thinking or emotion of your partner may lead to needless wrath and resentment. Let's say that Jenny purchased a new outfit with her spouse, John, for her date night. John's not commenting on how lovely she looks. He may believe that she looks lovely, but perhaps he assumes that she knows that already.

In the meanwhile, she assumes that he neither notices her effort nor likes how she appears, or maybe even disapproves of the money she spends on this outfit. Her feelings of hurt, anxiety and defensiveness fester all day. That may, of course, be avoided by instructing John to look lovely and by asking Jenny only, "How do I look?"

Let's say Anna always gets up in the middle of the night with the baby. Resentment grows as she assumes that it is Jeff's duty to do so. Meanwhile, Jeff assumes she wants to be the one with the baby since she's never told the other way. He would be glad to get up if she only asked. Telling your partner how you feel and checking his or her feelings is a key component of a successful relationship. If it doesn't come to you naturally, make a deliberate effort. The payout will make it valuable, and it will quickly become a precious way to remain connected.

Listen, Listen, So No Division

Just though you hear your partner talk doesn't imply that you listen. Concentrate your attention on the speaker. Keep good eye contact and body language responsive. Nothing indicates I don't want to look away and divert, or worse, to roll your eyes and cross your arms and legs. Put your telephone down and don't have several tasks while you're talking. Objectively listen, and try not to put words into the mouth of your partner. To paraphrase what you heard from the speaker simply to make sure that you didn't misunderstand anything.

Stop finding the fault

Criticism is a murderer of discussion. It is not beneficial to find faults in your partner, to criticise and point out everything he or she is doing wrong or might be doing differently. It's not your job to see what your partner can do otherwise. It's your job to see what you can do differently.

When it's hot, drop it

As I stated in chapter 1 of Brain Science 101, the brain on the bottom (primitive) is engaged when you are angry. This makes access to your upstairs (logical) brain harder. This isn't only for children. That's why we yell and then feel bad afterwards. We shout from our reflexive, primitive brain and then, when we can rationally think again, we understand that we shouldn't shout. When the discussion becomes hot, take a break to calm and wait until you feel the anger is gone, and you can think clearly and converse quietly. For calm-down methods, see Chapter 2.

Communicating with children

Over the years I have learned that the way I communicate with my children affects how they respond to me. Often they meet me in the same tone that I meet them. In other words, I receive what I give and want my children to learn that communication is polite and courteous in a related and loving connection.

One of the most practical methods of building good relationships is positive communication. Communication is not only the words we say, but the way we say them, our voice, our nonverbals, our conduct, and our written words. Contact the eye and give complete attention

You are essential to communicate as much as those real words, if not more so. The quiet treatment given to your child also sends you a message: "You are not right now worth my care and affection." Thus, we must not just be aware of the words that come out of our lips, but of all the methods in which we communicate.

Keep in mind what you already know to be true: the communication in which we communicate in our life is learned in childhood. This implies that you educate your child how to talk to each encounter. By learning her positive communication skills today, you can start her beneficial connections.

Respect

It is a common misunderstanding that we must talk sternly to children to listen to them. Parents frequently say, "My child won't listen if I don't cry!" If this is the case, then I'm concerned she has been trained to respond that. The sad fact is that the more frequently you use yelling and harsher words or tones to "make your child listen," the more often you will use them since they learn that they truly don't have to behave until you blow their head.

In way, she will learn how to communicate with others so that you may see her speaking with a sibling or other colleagues or even with you in the same hard or loud style.

Remember what I stated before, even if you don't feel loved, you can be loving. When your child is chilly, you may be warm. You can be calm when he's angry, nice and cruel. You're the grown-up. You're the model. The model. You can get your point through without the loud authoritative voice that you may have used to hear as you grew up. Yelling and threats tend to quiet off children. It puts people on the defensive and activates their lower reactive brain. Being polite doesn't give them the message you're not responsible for. It tells they are respected. You want your child to believe in herself, isn't it?

Encouragement and praise

A much was written about praise. Alfie Kohn did great research on this topic, and I will not try to explain his results in this book, but I am sure you will look at him if you want to study this topic further. What I will do is provide a brief summary of what is usually considered smart parenting in the positive parenting community.

Encouragement is good for children. It helps them flourish and flourish. "I believe you." "I believe you." "You could do that!" "Keep trying. Keep trying. You're going to figure it out, I'm sure." "You're doing well! Continue the excellent job."

Praise is also good as long as it is not hollow praise offered just to make the child work for you. It is best presented as a genuine appreciation and recognition of the effort of the child rather than just as an admiration of the result. "Thank you so much for having picked up your toys. It was extremely useful," the child provides something more than "Billy, good job." "It was an extremely challenging historical exam. You have studied hard and put the effort into it."

What it is all about is that it is a good time that the boy (1) is able to feel you are aware and know you recognise her, and appreciate her, and that (2) can make her own judgments on the quality of her work and not learn how to rely on everyone's approval to find pleasure.

Communication by condition

While someone hasn't spoken to you when he's angry or turns his back deliberately when you enter the room, you know how it pulses. It's not a good way to make a child behave. It is not a mature way to communicate and to give your child quiet treatment or cold shoulder, which is a bad example. This is love that is conditional. Love is not a prize, friends. Hugs, attention, love, nice words — they are no incentives provided to the child just when he does what he likes us and when he is pulled away. These are the lifelines of a child. They should always be provided without constraint or reluctance.

Language of the body

Language of the body is an integral component of communication, and may represent 50 percent or more. You say a lot without a word. You say a lot. Are you smiling when your child goes into the room? Sit up and make eye contact as she tells you about her day? In your body language alone, you may be aggressive, careful, bored, calm, open and much more. It makes sense to understand what type of body language is positive if you wish to communicate favourably. Positive messages are provided below:

- Strengthening

- Contact the eye

- Ignorance of distractions

- Slightly forward tilting your head

- Keep your arms and legs open and not crossed

- Making soft motions.

- smiling

- with a casual look

- nodding

Written Word Writings

The written word has a way to secret places in the heart in which speech is impossible. Do not underestimate the value of the timely letter of love and encouragement—in a lunch box, tucked into a bookpack at dinner, or laying on a pillow of your kid. A "Mom and Me" newspaper is also an excellent way to communicate so that your child can feel safe when sharing thoughts and feelings to you. Private journaling is a great way of working with thoughts and emotions for your school age or old child.

Styles of communication

Communicate in a way that refers to the child's age and interest. The following is a contour of communication techniques during the childhood phases.

Childhood: 0–12 monthly.

Children actively communicate with cries, sounds and nonverbal indicators, and how we perceive these indications is vital for stable attachment development. Nonverbal cues include facial expressions such as grins, grimacers, moves like kicking legs, and gestures like pointing, nodding, and shaking their heads. In addition, children squeal, laugh and babble to talk to carers. To encourage children to communicate:

- Speak and sing often to your baby. Respond to crying swiftly and warmly.

- Read to her many times. Perhaps she doesn't understand what you say, but she will like hearing your voice, which helps her to understand her early on.

- Copy her gestures and sounds. Hold a "conversation" with her by copying her verbal words and pausing to "respond."

- Use a pleasant, cheerful voice to chat to her.

- Show your baby interest when he laughs, babbles and coos. Look at her and respond to encourage her to continue with this communication.

- His facial expressions mirror.

- Engage your listening skills throughout the day by talking to her often.

In addition to crying, sounding and nonverbal information, children start communicating with language. To encourage communication and the development of language in young children:

- Always show attention and respond to communication attempts. This shows that you appreciate communication and models good communication skills.

- Interpret the gestures of your child. When he points to his cup of juice, say, "Oh, juice! You'd like juice!"

- Sportscast while playing your child. This strengthens grammar skills and helps the organisation of thinking. "You're on the track driving the train. A tunnel arrives here! You've passed the tunnel!" Encourage imaginative play. Children frequently express freely during pretending play. Join them in their inventive play.

- Eliminate negative comments such as "Trains don't go on roads" and "Grass's not red" while your child plays.

- Give your child a good emotion vocabulary by categorising and talking frequently about emotions.

- Discuss other people's feelings and expressions. "Do you see how the hands of Nathan cover his ears? Loud noise doesn't like it." This encourages children to search for non-verbal information and strengthens communication skills.

- Respect the feelings of your child. Even if you have to modify the behaviour, it is crucial to recognise and respect its emotions. Connect words to deeds. "I wash the toes!"

- Read your child. Read with your child. Encourage him to point and name what he sees. Let him turn the pages.

- Make requests explicit, age relevant and straightforward.

S–5 Yearc PrECGHOOLERC:

They're talking now! Preschoolers would like to chat a lot to try all their new skills. It is vital to create an atmosphere in which your child can openly talk about his thoughts, feelings and ideas. To encourage communication among pre-school students:

- Continue her imaginative play and offer plenty of free play opportunities with you or others.

- Just ask questions about your day, prior events, or how you feel. Provide descriptive terms if necessary.

- Encourage your child to express positive as well as negative emotions and give him the tools to express them properly.

- Read classical literature every day aloud.

- Keep talking about her emotions and teaching her problem solving skills.

- Pre-school preschoolers may ask "why" or "how" frequently. Don't reject these questions as irrelevant. Do your best to reply.

- Please give attention when your preschooler wants to communicate with you. Engage in active listening and summarise what you heard to your child.

- Nod, smile, be warm and fond of her. This helps her to feel valued and encourages communication to continue.

- Watch body language and behavioural indications. Pre-school preschoolers still can't explain what's wrong.

- Give your rules arguments. "We hold our hands in the car park so you won't get hit by a car." "If you ride your bike, you need to wear your helmet to protect your head if you fall off."

- Curb criticism and give much encouragement.

CGHOOL-AGE Children: Year 5–12

School children are beginning to look more complexly at the world. They think more logically and can reflect more. They also begin to ask challenging questions. To encourage communication amongst school age:

- Make an effort to spend quality time together, in which there are plenty of opportunities for open discussions.

- Ask precise questions rather than generic ones.

- Work together to resolve disputes. Ask your child how to solve the problem and let him have some say in the rules and results.

- Continue to encourage him to talk about positive and negative emotions.

- Don't interrupt your child. Do not interrupt your child. Allow him to finish before you respond. Children value this as much as adults do! Avoid critique.

- Show interest in the interests of your child. Ask questions and be truly curious about what he loves.

Questions for discussion

1. What habits of communication do you think you have taken up as a child?

2. What communication norm would you like to set for your children?

3. Did your parents communicate with you with respect? How did this change how you communicate with your child?

4. Do you tend to communicate under tendency — retain words and warmth while you are unpleasant?

5. Pay attention to the language of your body. What are you transmitting?

6. How can you make the way you communicate with your child?

Put it in practise

Positive communication becomes your natural way of communicating with your family through a little practise. I would remind you of the following points:

- Use statements of "I." Instead of saying, "You never help the children," try, "I would appreciate better assistance for the children." This doesn't immediately put your partner on the defensive.

- Look for solutions for win-win. Remember, throughout the chapter, the five-step process:

(1) separating a person from an issue,

(2) evaluating beliefs, emotions, and concerns,

(3) investigating, inventing, and rethinking options,

(4) settle for a solution with which you are both satisfied, and (5) give a fair trial solution.

- Drop the hypothesis. Assuming what your partner thinks or feels often results in unpleasant feelings or grief. The best thing is to ask.

- Objectively listen. Listen. We tend to think about the ideal answer to hear our thoughts. Rather, learn to listen carefully and to understand how your loved ones feel.

- Don't criticise the people of your family. Criticism is crumbling and we're encouraging and giving life.

- If you're angry, take a break. Don't keep talking till you're calm.

- Talk to your partner and children respectfully. You get what you give. What you give.

- Offer real encouragement and praise.

- In trying to discipline your child or get back to your partner, don't reject attention and affection. It is an untimely way of communicating your feelings.

- See the language of your body. Use this chapter's open, careful body language.

- Use written word. Use written word. In lunch boxes, lay love notes on pillows and jokes.

Try the exercises below to develop communication skills.

Three-Minute Listening Challenge

Four to eight index cards, each with a topic written on it, are required. Divide the family into pairs, each consisting of a speaker and a listener. The speaker selects a card blindly and talks about the topic for three minutes. During this time, the listener cannot speak. Three minutes later, the listener must summarise the speaker without consent, disagreement or discussion. The speaker and listener then change roles.

The advantage: Part of effective communication is listening and understanding, not just responding. This workout increases the ability to listen

As the listener needs to accurately sum up what the speaker is saying so he or she really needs to pay attention, empathy and intention.

Obstacle Running

Create an obstacle course with scattered furniture (chairs, cushions, etc) and divide the family into pairs. The sighted partner must take the person safely to the other side of the room via the obstacle course. The blindfolded person must only utilise his or her listening skills to avoid objects.

The advantage: This practise increases confidence and listening skills.

Calm acting

In this game, two people will have a chat, but only one is allowed to speak. Person A is going to speak its part when person B is going to communicate its lines nonverbally.

Give each person a copy of the script:

A: You saw my notebook? I don't know where I left. I don't know where I left. B: What notebook is available?

A: blue one. A: blue one. Yesterday, I let you borrow it. B: That's it?

A: No. No. That's red. That's red. This is the one you have borrowed. B: I didn't! I didn't!

A. It might be under the couch. Are you going to look? B: Certainly. Give me a minute. Give me a minute.

A: How long will it take?

B: Have a go! You're really excited. When you're domineering, I dislike. A: Forget it. Forget it. I will discover it myself. I will find it myself.

B: Wait! Wait! It's here! I found it! I found it!

Benefit: This exercise shows how without uttering a word we may communicate a lot!

Now give person B a secret feeling, such nervousness, boredness, or excitement, to act while communicating its line. Guess what emotion affects person B. Have a person

Bonus advantage: this exercise improves emotional intelligence, showing how our emotions can affect our behaviour, and how it is communicated even when we don't speak to people.

Notes of Appreciation

List three actions every family member has recently done that make you feel loved. Ask them to do the same thing. Write each list for each person on a separate letter and then exchange and relax in a loved and appreciated feeling. Start an appreciation board to make a daily habit of noticing the good. We're using a dry-erase board. Encourage each family member to write something on the board before night and watch positive feelings bloo

Chapter 8
BUILDING A FOUNDATION OF TRUST

Trust is the fruit of a relationship in which you know you are loved.
—William P. Young

CONNECTION AND TRUST is the foundation for building your relationship with your child. This connection foundation is based on one of the key principles of positive parental relationships: attachment. Lovingly and regularly satisfying the needs of your child has a long-term and positive impact on the development of your brain. When a child feels confident that his caregiver satisfies his needs, his brain is ready to learn. Then he is free to explore his world. However, without secure attachment, learning is inhibited because primary needs are being met.

There are several benefits to secure attachment that include improved childhood and adult relationships, higher empathy, better emotional health, less anxiety, increased attention support, greater creativity and better ability to cope with ups and downs of the life. Research has revealed that the best potential foundation for good emotional, intellectual, physical and social development is secure attachment.

Create trust with your infant

From the start, children learn to trust or not trust the world. You, the caregiver, shape your perception of the world. If you always meet the basic needs of the infant for food, love and attention, she learns to trust. Moreover, children make their value on the basis of the signals based from you and other caregivers. Of course, you want that "You are valuable" message, a message that she will be taking with her throughout her life, ingrained in her self-image. Indeed, an excellent present for your child is a secure attachment.

Building trust and connection with your child:

- Get to know the cues of your child and respond quickly.

- Feed her at the earliest hunger signs, if possible before she starts crying. Talk quietly and make eye contact as you feed her.

- Smile, talk, and connect with your baby frequently.

- Give plenty of hugs, kisses, skin-to-skin contact and snuggles. Respond to cries swiftly. Don't let your baby cry alone. Parenthood at night is exhausting, but vital. Infants must be parented back to sleep. If you wake up often and need support, there are mild ways of teaching better sleep. Look for peaceful sleep remedies from Elizabeth Pantley.

Create your trust or preschool trust

Toddlerhood is the time when children become conscious of themselves. Your toddler is now beginning to understand that he is separate from others and independent. He will need you to be his home base while he explores his world further.

Follow these trustworthy and secure relationship standards during these years:

- Practice what you teach. What you preach. Even little children can detect if you're not sincere. Remember, your example is more important than your words.

- Listen to the minor stuff now so later he will tell you the great stuff. You might not be very interested in hearing what happened

- Pre-school or why a specific toy is so great, but show nonetheless interest. In these early years, you create the foundation for respectful communication.

- Be honest. Be honest. It's tempting to say that when you really are too busy to take him, the park is closed, but honesty is always the best policy. He's young, not smart. Respect him sufficiently to tell him the truth. Wouldn't you want the same thing?

- Keep your promises. Keep your promises. If yousay telling him to lie down for an extra tale tonight at bedtime, make sure you follow through. Your word is currently important because you want to know that his word is important later—so you teach the value to keep your promises. Don't make anything that you can't keep.

- Praise the process, not the result. You want to send the message that it's important to try and not get it perfect. "You really work hard to fit those puzzle pieces!" This teaches the worth of effort and creates a connection when you take the time to stop and recognise your child.

- Hours and schedules are important. In Chapter 6, we will talk more about this. This gives young children a sense of safety.

Middle Childhood Building Trust

Between early and middle childhood a huge amount of development and growth occurs. Middle childhood is when the components of the brain which mediate emotional and social learning are primed. Your 5-12-years-old shows more independence and comprehension of her role in the world, and she begins to ponder about her future.

Self-concept is still evolving and her connection with you is still crucial, but it is increasingly independent.

Here is how to keep trust and connection in childhood:

- Show interest in what your child is interested in. Join her in her world. Join her in her world. Don't make exaggerated; they only disconnect. Make sure that she knows the rules and the penalties of breaking rules. This eliminates the need to threaten totally. An instance of a

- "If you don't take these toys now, they're going into the garbage!," is the overblown threat. This will not trigger cooperation, and will you truly toss it away?

- Don't overact. Don't overact. Keep your emotions and answers in line with the scenario. Making mountains out of molehills can only result you strain from unneeded mountains. Very few things are a crisis, and some terrible choices don't make horrible people.

- Show your faith. Show faith. Know that your child has faith in her. This is essential for her to have faith in herself.

- Keep privacy. If your daughter tells a secret to you, keep it there. Don't breach her trust by blurring her secret with another friend or family member, except there is danger, of course. Children require a trustworthy person and you want that person to be you.

- Children of this age care about their peers' opinions. It's better not to correct your child in front of her peers, but to pull it out and whisper it in her ear, or save it later if possible. It's awkward to be called before your pals, which can lead to mistrust and disconnection.

- Connect by telling your childhood stories. Children of this age are interested in hearing about the time you have spent anything similar to what you are doing and how you managed it. This also helps them to better know you.

Building your Teen Trust

Teens may look grown up, but remember that their brain growth is still going on until the way-twenties. If you have a teenager, I highly recommend Dr. Dan Siegel's Brainctorm book. Although this is a time to let go in many respects, you must never start up trust and connection.

Here are some recommendations for maintaining a healthy and strong trust and connection during teen years.

Keep a communication line open. It is therefore important that, during the years, you listened to these small things and set an example of honesty and integrity in your speech and perhaps you had a long-established practise of listening, without a fast judgement.

Convey trust. It's still important to show your child faith. If you make him know you believe in him, his self-esteem will boost, which may always use a boost in these years.

Be respectful of your space and privacy requirements.

Respect your views and don't play down your concerns. He needs you to set an example of how others listen and respect, which builds healthy connections.

If in early years you create this foundation well, it will be much easier to build on it as the years go by. If, for whatever reason, a secure connection in the early years has been missed, just start where you are and build the most of it. Store a great deal of grace—for yourself and your child—to tap in turbulent times and trials. If breaks occur, reconnect as quickly as feasible. If trust is broken, try to change it. As an adult, it will always be your obligation to re-connect and mend. It is always the responsibility of the maturer mind to reach and lead the way in the first place.

Questions for discussion

- Do you feel you have a strong connection with your own parents? Did you have confidence in them? Do you feel they have confidence in you?

- Might you understand how your trust or mistrust, connection or disconnection with your own parents can get into your current relationship to your own child?

- How do you plan to build your child's trust and connection from now on

Chapter 9
DEFINING YOUR FAMILY CULTURE

What is more important to our spirits than to feel united for life—to be with one another in silent, ineffable memories? The expectations, habits, roles and more of George Eliot. We usually see only countries or vast populations as cultures, but sociologists say that even individual families have cultures of their own, and research has shown that the culture of family can play a more important role in shaping a child than parenting. 11 Family cultures are powerful, forming the world of children, and the type of culture a family generates strongly predicts the joy of a child. Blessed families deliberately establish positive family cultures. Parents who don't deliberately establish a family culture — who don't think much about the values they want to inculcate and the ties they want to establish and don't plan to build a family — will fall into a faulty culture that is haphazardly created in the years that pass.

Seven Family Culture Pillars

1. Values

Examples are family values like integrity, respect, honesty, mutual responsibility and the wider community. They're going to learn what you live. It is unproductive to say that respect is a family value if disregard is routinely demonstrated in the home.

These values should be kept in order to become simply a way to be and relate. Your values (more on this later) are stated in your mission statement so put it in a conspicuous position and talk about them consistently. Live these values regularly, more importantly.

2. Dispositions

In the Oxford DIGTIONARY the word dicpociation is defined as "a person's inherent quality of mind and nature," with the synonyms of GHARAGTER, temperament and mentality. I also believe that this includes attitude and self-esteem. Let's break this into bits in bite-size.

What is your nature? What is your character? Is that your partner? What about your mind's quality? Are you positive or negative – half-full or half-empty glass? Your temperament, what about it? Are you usually calm and relaxed or tighter wounded? Are you angry easily or can you let things go? Are you easy to keep up with? You're a perfectionist? Do you think about yourself favourably or do you have weak self-esteem?

All these things play in your children's environment and are part of the family culture jigsaw. You and your partner may probably have different answers to these questions. My hubby is more positive and relaxed. I'm more a perfectionist and thrown away readily. Our children have taken up our varied traits and characteristics. Just like me, one child is more worried. The other, like Dad, is happy-go-lucky. Have they inherited or learned these traits? I don't know—maybe a bit of both. The point is that it is important to learn and respect each other and to discover ways of living in harmony for all of the various provisions in the home.

Did you know it can be contagious self-esteem? "Is Low Self-Esteem Contagious in an article?" "Research published in Perconality Journal and COGIAL PCYGHOLOGY reveals that while Katie Hurley says, "

Positive re-framing from friends and loved ones can increase self esteem in people battling with low self esteem and can make them feel more comfortable with low self-esteem. This indicates that self-esteem can be contagious. Of course, the other side is that positivity may also be contagious." 12 It is therefore important to take good care of yourself and perform the effort you need to become a positive person. Being a positive parent is lot easier if you feel positive!

3. Executive expectations

This is a somewhat large topic that goes beyond your children's expectations and beyond the scope of this book, but here I will try to sum it it.

Yes, what you expect is very important about your children, and I don't just mean to expect him to clean his room. I'm talking about expecting for him to be a good person, to be able to meet obstacles and to make intelligent judgments and learn from impoverished people.

This includes your partner's expectations, as it provides an example of what your children will one day expect from theirs.

It teaches kids about the roles of gender, which impact how people of the opposite sex treat themselves and how they treat people of the same sex.

Children learn your expectations about society, people from different cultures and ethnicities, employers and jobs, governments, politicians, restaurant servers and battleshipers beyond relationship expectations. You learn what you expect of shortage or wealth, misfortune or good, difficulty or blessing. Your expectations are often carried over to your children and you suddenly have a full house of expectations, and these expectations play an important part in your family culture.

4.   Habits

Like everything else, our children pick up our habits—the good, the bad. Has anyone a habit of yelling? It is not difficult to see how this influences the culture of the family. It is also influenced by the habit of having dinner numerous times a week. Try forming and/or maintaining positive habits; if you don't want your kids to take them, it is best that you drop them. This pertains just to habits, as in general, children take up the most things they eat, including cheetos and possibly crumbs of cat food, and often eat what they eat. Only a fair warning.

5.   Communication

We have gone beyond communication a lot in this book because this is so crucial for building strong family ties, therefore it makes sense that it is also crucial for your family culture. Which family is gladder, who utilises positive, reverent communication or who criticises, criticises and shouts? Positive communication naturally generates positive links, therefore the communication skills are working on.

6.   Resolution of conflicts

This is a part of communication but in building a positive family culture it is so important that it needs to be debated. It is vitally crucial that you model, teach and expect peaceful conflict resolution to your child in the home. When you put numerous personalities under one roof, conflict will occur, and what you do with it can really make or break a relationship.

Steps towards a peaceful resolution of conflicts:

- Learn how to detect and manage emotions for children.

- Use time to bring the small child to a safe, relaxing place and learn how to calm before talking a solution. The time-in in chapter 9 is discussed.

- Older children can take the place of a peace table (see chapter 9) order a peace circle about seven years old.

- Teach positive (e.g. "I") communication and not blaming.

7. Traditions

Rituals and traditions strengthen the family and let children feel that they are part of something greater than themselves. In the last chapter, daily routines were discussed and play an important role in your family culture. Weekly rituals such as family film night or pizza night, spiritual service and family gatherings will bring life to your family plan. Birthdays, holidays, meetings and celebrations all place a building block of your deliberately positive family culture.

Create your family model

You'd not just take the random materials and start to throw them together if you were to build a house. You would have to have a blueprint. The same goes for building a family culture. Drawing a blueprint or mission statement will assist you in defining your goals and define you of your future vision. To deliberately build the family that your heart wants, you need to know exactly what materials are needed and how you are going to put them together.

Your family plan sets your goals, designs a plan to attain those goals and implements this plan with step-by-step achievements to reach them. While you and your partner are in part of drafting this mission statement, each family member should participate in drawing up this statement. Everyone feels invested in this. Uniting around a same set of goals will build the connection between your family.

The benefits of a plan

A good mission statement will define your family members and motivate them. As already indicated, it will connect the family in a common set of goals. Everyone in the family has a voice in drafting a blueprint and creates solidarity. Decision-making is easy since you know what is not for the purpose of your family. As you draught your blueprint, each family member starts to begin his or her values, beliefs, ambitions, goals, and vision. Finally, the blueprint will become a 'code of behaviour,' which you can refer your children a tool for teaching.

Your legacy starts here

Lately, I have been giving a lot about what my legacy will be. How will my children speak to their children and grandchildren about me? For what am I going to be remembered? Similarly, how do community people see our family? How did we make our contributions? I hope to remember him as a woman who freely and unconditionally gave love and had a positive impact on her surroundings. I hope the legacy of my family is one of gentle kindness and sincerity. What do you hope from your legacy?

Eventually your family blueprint will become your family legacy. Draft it very carefully. If you are set on the goals you write down and see them realise, you will leave a legacy of which you are proud. The truth is that in this world, we all leave our marks. We are all

Your family plan will be

Just leave some sort of legacy; not everybody leaves a good legacy. I know you want to leave a positive personal and family legacy for decades to come that will whisper your good reputation. Every step of the way, your family plan will guide you.

Drafting your blueprint

Your blueprint will be a family discussion on your values, beliefs, morality, dreams and goals. Each family member needs to engage in a discourse in order to succeed in this blueprint. It is important for everyone to be heard and respected when they give their thoughts.

Write down the answers of each person as you go. In this discussion, even very young children should be present. This is where they begin to learn the importance of the family unit and understand it.

To start with a list of values is useful. Our family values include time, learning, unity, tenderness, patience and presence, for example. Enter all the values in the list of your family members. You can set them to the most important and pleasant time for everyone, after compiling a good, hardy list.

List your beliefs next. Whether you are religious or not, you certainly have strong beliefs about the meaning of life and how people should be treated and so on. My family, for example, thinks that everyone deserves respect and kindness. We trust that orphans and children are cared for in poverty. We believe in aiding needy animals and lovingly caring for animals.

Finally, individually and as a family, list your goals. From building greater self-control, getting the team to bringing emotionally intelligent children or beginning your own business – write it down, together with everyone else's ideas, regardless of what you want for yourself and your family.

Once you have a full list of values, beliefs and goals, host a gathering to really shed light on your family's mission. Place the final product, have it signed by each family member and write it highly noticeable somewhere. Refer to it as often and at least once a month.

With your family growing and children growing up, your mission is worth reviewing and reviewing annually. This is a way to renew the vision and keep all on the same page.

Now that you know what you want to build, it's time to see how to build it. This is where you will grow like a flow chart on your blueprint. Take every value and write down how you can live it. Your entries may look like this, for example:

- Clownecc: We're not going to accept too many EXTRAGURRIGULAR AGTIVITIEC and we're going to enjoy a lot of downtime together.

- Gentlenecc: Harch wordc or AGTIONC will not be tolerated. If a family member treats a family member in a non-smooth way, it is this perconic recponcibility to repair the relationship chip and do something like this.

- Do the same with your beliefs. How are you going to live according to your beliefs?

- We believe in the earth's GARING. In our GOMMUNITY ONGE a month, we'll be rEGYGLE, GONCERVE, and PIGK up trach.

- We believe all kindnecc animal decerve. ONGE, we volunteer in the animal chelter every three months. We are going to take blanketc and other items to the chelter in the winter. We shall tenderly GARe for our own petc.

Finally, do the same for your goals.

I want to make the team of baceball. Every day I PRAGTIGE and acknowledge the GOAGH ADVIGE.

When they're adults, I want to have a strong relationship with my GHILDRen. I'm going to chow them RECPEGT and UNGONDITIONAL love as they develop, and they're going to trust me BAGK as soon as they grow.

I want to have a dynamic marriage. I'll GOMMIT every day to EFFEGTIVE GOMMUNIGATION and to chow my love. I'll ENRIGH our FOGUCED Time Relationship together.

Here are a few questions to start developing your own family blueprint.

- What family do we want to be?

- What values are we going to maintain?

- What kind of atmosphere in our home do we want?

- What type of connections do we want to have?

- Who gives us inspiration and why?

Routines and rituals value

Your family culture can be drawn up at the table, but it is formed into everyday life. Routines and rituals are essential aspects in your culture. Children thrive with routines that are regular, consistent and predictable. Routines assist children to feel secure and emotionally stable as they learn that they can trust the adults. This frees them from playing and investigating their "work." Routines should be convenient and flexible—more like a daily flow than a tight timetable every day. As children learn their daily routine, they begin to understand what is important and what is important for the family. It teaches responsibility and how to handle themselves and their space positively.

Consistent daily routines can help children cope with stressful situations, such as sibling birth or moving to a new place. Additional advantages of routines include teaching young children good cleanliness habits, such as tooth and handwash, development of basic skills, time management and the establishment of body clocks. Children with a predictable bedtime routine tend to sleep more readily at time than children with no regular routines.

Your family is different and the routines you set are as unique as you are. If you find that a routine doesn't work, be flexible and work with your family to make it effective. Here are some ideas for routines throughout childhood.

Infants

Infants do not need a set routine. When they are hungry, we should feed them and let them sleep nap. They automatically create a kind of routine over time, and all we need to do is to help them make their quarters pleasant and sleep-friendly and feed them in an easy and predictable way. Finally, you may use the natural schedule of your child to build a routine that works for her and for the entire family.

Children and pre-school children

In particular, toddlers and pre-preschoolers thrive on routines. This is a good time to construct a visual chart or poster to guide you through your day. Use both photographs and written words to complete and refer to this chart often all day long. There can be anything like this in your daily flow:

- get dressed brush teeth playtime cleanup lunch

- Free play music dinner bath storey cleanup bedtime

Make it fun for your child by building minor rituals into your routines. Singing a morning song while dressing or specific bath rituals will make your day more enjoyable. Giving advance notice of transition to your toddler is respectful and helpful in reducing meltdowns. "In ten minutes we're going to leave the park." "We've got five minutes left, and then we go." "All right, time to go. Let's just race to the car!"

Another example of routine transition is when your child is taken away in school or childcare. You may sing the same song every day on your journey to the establishment, skip to the front door, give a hug and kiss, say the same rhyme or catchphrase (for way, "Later See you, Alligator") and wake up with a smile. This predictable little ritual lets your child start her day with positive feelings.

Children of school age

Children of school age can take greater responsibility for themselves and their environment. Routines around school mornings, homework, hobbies/sports, clean-up, jobs and bedding can be helpful.

Setting routines around these specific daily activities reduces stress. For example, it is likely that having a dedicated homework place and a set time to begin every day would reduce disagreements about doing that, especially if you are consistent, courteous and factual. Some children want to have charts to tick. Setting these routines with the input of your child will enhance collaboration.

Adolescents

Teenagers should be able to manage their routines with minimum supervision. They may still need aid and instruction, but they should in general now be well adapted to the family routines.

Rituals

I discussed building earlier in tiny rituals like singing in the morning when dressing or on the way to school. Rituals are the warm memories your child looks back and cherishes for a lifetime. "The purpose of rituals is connection. Becky Bailey, PhD, adds. Rituals create sacred space for oneness and unity." Anything you do together again and again, like a walk after dinner or waffles on a Sunday, is a ritual. You have probably built various rituals, and they provide your child a number of benefits. Dr Steven Wolin, a George Washington University psychiatrist, adds, "You will be more resilient as an adult if you grow up in a family of strong rituals." 1s Researchers have also discovered that children with family rituals are mentally better off in times of difficulty. You know at least that you create a common identity and a sense of order and belonging.

Here are some ideas to encourage your creativity in developing rituals for your family.

Every year on his birthday, my hubby got up and put butter on his nose, a family member. As strange as it seems, for him it's a cherished memory. However, we've not followed the tradition of butter, but we've made rituals for birthdays that include a lot of balloons and crepe paper – covered doors. How can you make your loved one's day special?

I blow up several white balloons as Halloween approaches and sketch fantasy faces on them. I've hung them out of our home and we get our ghost-hunting equipment and pop some ghosts just as it becomes dark.

The Christmas season is full with rituals, including collecting old toys and the home of ever-disastering gingerbread.

I grew up in Scrabble and Boggle's continuous diet. Family game night is an excellent idea, but it isn't so easy in our busy lives. Plan and switch it off, except it is part of the game, anything that dings, rings, or buzzes!

Bedtime storybooks are fantastic, but my boys are looking for a fabricated animated adventure. The space projection from the nightlight inspired many unforgettable journeys when we uncovered treasures, vanquished monsters and aliens and located new worlds!

Our countdown for New Year's Eve is made up of balloons with written activities that we pop up every hour, a tournament-style annual minute for winning it and too much confetti.

It is a good idea to build rituals around the transition of the year, such as back-to-school and seasonal rituals. In the spring, plant seeds. In the summer, go camping. In the fall, visit a pumpkin patch. In the winter go sledding.

Unplug every evening for a certain length of time. No phones or tablets permitted! Being able to rely on this quality time every day will be wonderful for your children and your family.

Peace culture—Taming Sibling Rivalry

When I bore my second child, for the first time in my life, I threw myself into the complexity of a sibling relationship very abruptly. As a child alone, I had fantastic ideas about living in peace with a best friend. Maybe, as I did, you envisioned your kids would be best friends, play together, knit, walk hand in hand. But then reality hit and you became the arbiter in continuous sibling conflicts. In the sake of "normal," you don't have to tolerate sibling rivalry. Certainly, it is not typical for children living under the same roof to argue occasionally, but it is important to cultivate strong sibling ties to maintain peace and create a positive family culture. Intentionally, it is important to minimise sibling rivalry, teach your children how to relate positively and offer an environment that will allow their relationship to grow.

When it comes to sibling rivalry, parents often reluctantly start the fire that we've been doing for days and years. I certainly made my share of fuelling rivalry mistakes. Since then, I have also learned how to create more peace. I'm going to share my mistakes and achievements in creating a culture of peace among my children in this part.

Error No. 1: Compare

I knew comparing my children wasn't a brilliant idea, but sometimes it's difficult to make a comparison. "Your brother has now been potty trained. Why do you make it hard?" How helpful was that in both teaching his brother to use the restroom and creating warm and flirting feelings? If you're not at all helpful, you're right.

Comparisons may have two results. One is anxiety over the "better" sibling, and the other a feeling of insufficiency or poor conception of oneself. Even if you make the "favourable" comparison – telling her, for example, that she is far more responsible than her sibling – this creates a competitive atmosphere. "The trouble is that comparisons strengthen the way we think about our children and consequently impact the way we treat them. Dr. Laura Markham, author of PEAGEFUL Parent of Happy Ciblingc, says: Perhaps even worse, any comparison we make might encourage our children to compare." 14 Install what you observe, what you like, what you want to alter, or what you have to do, rather than compare, but leave the other children out. Instead, describe what needs to be done "Why can you not finish your homework without fuss like your brother?" "You have homework to complete before television time."

Error No. 2: Labeling

When you grew up, were you and your siblings labelled? Was it publicly accepted that you were 'the clever' or 'the beautiful'

One talented?" It appears that I unintentionally labelled "the funny one" one of my boys. I wasn't saying, "Hey, you're funny, and that's not your brother!" It seemed to happen very surreptitiously because I laughed more at him and told things like, "You're so funny!" His brother almost always would chime up, "Am I too funny?" Then he often tried to "measure" performance to make us laugh precisely like that.

This is a hard scenario, because how can a parent acknowledge one child's skills and achievements without feeding the competition? I believe that the key is to make that every child feels as loved, valued and good about himself. Our solution is not to stop laughing at the hilariousness of my child, but to identify something about his brother that we have brought to light and appreciated equally.

Victory No. 1: Bond Recognition

I noticed and mentioned when my boys were friendly or good at each other. Something needs to be spoken to talk about what you want in your life. I read this about positivism in several papers and it turns out that it works incredibly effectively. You get more of what you FOGUC on. I received more of it when I focused on their rivalry. Things improved dramatically when I focused on their connection.

Victory No. 2: Creating a team environment

We are a team in my family and we work as a team instead of fighting for stars or check marks. We have a team chart instead of individual task charts. Weekly family gatherings are helpful in the atmosphere of a team. At our meetings, we all get equal opportunities to assess any challenges we face and plan our holidays, etc. In engaging siblings in celebrating each other, for example by helping to watch a birthday party of a brother or sister or watching the performance of a sibling, the message is, "We are all together here." Family rituals and routines promote the atmosphere of a team/family.

Victory No. 3: Set clear boundaries

Children deserve to be comfortable and protected in their own homes, and unregulated sibling rivalry can make a home feel like a safe haven. I don't expect my kids to get along always or to enjoy each other, but I expect them to avoid violence, mocking or calling by names. I expect their disagreements to be respectful. This is a limit I have made for them. Set suitable limits, which respect every person in the home and create an atmosphere of acceptance and love, not rivalry and conflict.

When siblings argue, it will be your ruling whether to step. You're not always going to have to go to the rescue. Give them time to work on it, but step in if it escalates physically and verbally into violence. All children must be taught fundamental skills in conflict mediation. Teach to speak with respect, utilise the statements of "I" and take a break when things get heated like you learned to do in chapter 4. However, realise that these skills require time and age to develop. These are brain functions upstairs such that young children cannot always have this kind of logic and reasoning. It's still good to talk about it and to practise it, but expect a long time until they perfect it. Keep your bounds and teaching, and don't be disheartened. (In Chapter 9 I explore restriction establishment and enforcement.) Many adults still struggle with communication and peaceful resolution of conflicts, so that your children can begin their early teaching. What a difference for the future we parents can make!

Questions for discussion

What's your temperament? What is your partner? What is it? Is your child? How can respect and tolerance be promoted?

Are your values in sync with your expectations, habits and attitudes?

What does your family do periodically to make routine operation easier and more smooth?

What prevents you from creating a consistent routine if anything?

List at least five rituals you wish to be a part of the culture of your family.

Are you comparing your children to each other occasionally? Talk about how you can deliberately keep comparisons that rivalry with fuel.

Searching and recognising positive sibling interactions is important. Do you already do this? Do you want to make a point of making it daily and notice changes for at least one week?

Put it in practise

The foundation of the family life you want is founded on your vision and the trust and connection that you and your children establish. You put your vision on paper when you create your blueprint for the family to view. Because everyone participates in its part, your blueprint is the vision for the whole family, giving all the guidance and goals. Talk frequently about your blueprint. Family meetings are a good time to review at them. It will not serve its purpose if you create it and put it in a drawer. It must be discussed and lived every day, often highlighted in family gatherings, and if you correct your child to remain out of touch with what is set. Bring your blueprint in a major place in the home and talk about it often will help shape your family and fulfil your dreams.

Stay in a prominent place, visible to anyone, in your blueprint.

At family gatherings, review your blueprint at least once a month.

Concentrate your plan while correcting. 3. "Our family mission statement says, for example, that we treat one other with kindness. It's not nice to say he's dumb to your brother. We did not agree to treat one other like this."

Take the five rituals described in question 5 and develop a plan to get started immediately. For example, if you want to create a family game night tradition, go ahead and plan one for the next weekend. Buy an online board game or look for games your family would like to enjoy. Your attitude towards the new tradition will bring, thus

When you reveal the plan to your family, show enthusiasm and your positive at the table.

If you have a problem with rivalry in your home, I recommend Ciblingc Without Rivalry by Adele Faber and Elaine Mazlish and Happy Ciblingc, by Dr Laura Markham, the aforementioned PEAGEFUL Parent. Here are a few measures to begin a peace turnaround.

Take care of your words and actions so that you do not create any unwitting rivalry.

Find something to celebrate about every child.

Set explicit limits on physical and mental violence. While there are discrepancies, the reason for naming, hostility or bullying of any kind is never good, so be sure that these things will not be accepted in the home. Refer to Chapter 9 for ideas on punishable limit enforcement.

Not only are great moments in life that define your family and influence your children, but they are also ordinary everyday moments. They are their environment, their family traditions, their connections and their daily routines. How fortunate are our children that parents lovingly and deliberately create positive family cultures, healthy relationships and happy days. We create lovely kindergartens. Every day, there is not much glamour in showing up for bedtime, kissing scrapes, cleaning nose and comforting parents, but work is not more important than parent work since you help build a brighter future for the human race.

One method that I use to concentrate on my goals is to write three intentions a day to start my day. I keep it in front of a binder and keep it on my kitchen table, which I go through several times a day, with my binder. Keep your intentions brief, concise, purposeful and fully feasible. Think about your day ahead and what to do to make your home feel calm and peaceful. Here are a few samples to start you.

I'm going to spend at least 10 minutes in children's play with no interruptions.

Before I respond to an exciting event, I will take deep breaths.

I'm going to say how much I appreciate it today to my hubby.

I'm going to spend a little additional one-on-one time today with my child. I'm not going to sign up in social media till my children are in bed. I'm not going to sit on the park bench. I'm going to play with my kids. This evening, I'll do something romantic for my partner.

Today I shall feed myself on nutritional food, not on the children's plates.

I'm going to exercise today for at least s0 minutes.

I'm not going to allow bad thoughts to stay in my mind. Today I'm going to choose love.

Tonight, I'm going to treat myself to a warm bath and soft music. Today, I choose to be cheerful.

Chapter 10

SEEING CHILDREN IN A NEW WAY

I was emotional. I was emotional. I felt sad and overwhelmed and for days. Finally, I could no longer fight back the tears. My deux boys were busy playing super-heroes, so I walked into my bedroom, sunk on the other side of the bed, where I thought I was going to be concealed from vision if the adventure of my super-heroes brought them through my door. The tears flowed till my nose was swollen and my eyes puffy. My 6-year-old arrived in the room and saw my expression. He took his mask off, lay his sword upon his bed, sat next to me and just put his arms around me without saying a word. He held me for a few minutes and spoke all that was to be said at that moment with his lovely eyes and a soft embrace. This is a child's true heart.

I haven't always seen his lovely heart. I had a very different storey just three years before. I have been focused so much on his misconduct that I miss the compassion he has for all people and animals and the brightness shining in his delicate spirit. I've been correcting him for my days, placing him over and over in time. I thought every violation had to be addressed, or he would think he could get away with bad behaviour. That was true, I was warned. So our days were full with tears and struggle, and I missed tremendously the love connection that I shared with him as he was an infant. I only hoped to hold it in my lap, rock it again, brush his hair and wrap his arms around me. However, we were there, fighting for control, more

Disconnected as ever. My heart broke, and I began to look for answers—responses that led me to positive parenthood.

For six years now, I have been parenting this way, not flawlessly but consistently. However, when my sons are showing childlike behaviour in public, their laughter grows too loud, and I feel the stars of foreigners around me, I can feel my cheeks blush and the need to swiftly stop them. Then, I remember it's all right for children to be kids. Perhaps, if we'd all be more childlike — if we'd laughed a little louder, played a little harder, noticed with wonder the wind in our faces and taken the time to say that it feels nice, if we could slow down our fast-paced adult lives and watch a child's eyes again—perhaps then we would be a child.

I realised that children do not have negative intentions into this world. You can't tyre us out, test our patience, or push us across the line. You come to us with a longing for love, connection and

belonging. However, we have been taught to only get them from complying with our rules and following our directives. These things we don't give freely. What if we did? What if we did? What if we met their human hearts' needs and never threatened to sweep them away? Imagine a satisfied generation of hearts!

Imagine a world in which we can perceive children in a different perspective.

And what if we looked at them with the

same emotion and wonder as when they were put in our arms for the first time? What if we did not let "terrible twos" advertisements and other scary messages to enter our minds and alter our perceptions?

Can we see the motives of our children as pure and not conniving? Can we see our children as blessings, love and learn here? We can do this if we wish to perceive them. Our children's perception impacts how we deal with them.

Unfortunately, the way we view children in our culture made us relate poorly to them. We perceive attention in searching where there's but a want to link, clinginess where there's only a reason for love, disobedience, and defiance where there is only a will to learn.

It's just a need to expand. We view them as manipulating, sympathetic and egoistic and base our relationships with them on these notions.

We tend to reduce children to nothing but their behaviour.

Children are more than their night sleep ability. They are more than willing to obey immediately. It's more than just a grade. It's more than a feeling. They are more than the behaviour they portray on the surface at any one time. They are human beings—beautiful and untidy, wild and caring, worth knowing, not merely thinking about.

Let's take a closer look today at what it means to be a child, not just what it takes to raise a child.

Let's take a deeper look at what it means to be a GHILD today and not just what raice takes!

Society expects children to act as mature young adults, and this unreasonable expectation is putting unnecessary pressure on parents to make their children, especially publicly, perform well. Children aren't tiny adults. Their brains have a great deal to do. We often punish you

They have no control over anything: an undeveloped brain. We presume they have nasty intentions when they don't actually have them.

It is enormous disappointment when children are expected to act like adults when they act like children. Many parents are, it appears, comfortable talking to their presence with other parents, sometimes even with their children. This makes them feel better, parents say, as though they're not alone. But do they cease thinking how the child feels? I wonder, though.

Recently, in the presence of children, I have overheard the following statements:

- "I can't wait to start school," one mom stated. "He's been driving me insane all summer!" Her son stood next to her, watching the floor down.

- "Is your baby good? Gosh, mine isn't! Mine isn't! He's a whiny baby," said a toddler's mother in the waiting room of the paediatrician.

- "Mine are rotten brats," a mother informed the check-out lady. Her children sat in the waggon, hearing the message clearly and loudly.

- None of these children spoke a word. None of them said, "Wow, mom. It damages my feelings."

Just because children communicate not enough to express their sense of severe disgrace or hurt vocally does not mean that they feel it.

Why do we think it okay to speak to and about our children in their presence so terribly? Do we not think they understand? How can we expect kids to understand more sophisticated ideas like social property, if they cannot understand cuts such as, "mine are spoiled brats." Or do we think our harsh words will motivate them somehow? Again, it's playing cultural conditioning. It is unfortunately culturally accepted to treat children in this way. In fact, it is almost expected to whine about the annoyance of our kids and the sacrifice that we have to make for them. It seems that this is one way we strengthen the bonding between parents. However, I disagree the premise that it will motivate them in their presence to be better children. If shaming is always a motivation, it is at a heavy cost.

Dr. Brené Brown has been exploring shame, guilt and vulnerability for the past 12 years. She writes in her book The Giftc of IMPERFEGTION15, "Shame, shame, disrespect, betrayal, and withholding affection are damaging to the origins of love." Those words to cut? They're destructive. They're damaging. And she remarks very sadly, "Shame is corroding the exact part of us that we think we can fix."

That's big. That is worthy of our attention.

Children, like everyone else, feel most cooperative when treated with respect and care. Adults do not respond well to people who speak rudely to us or treat us with disrespect. Is it a long way to think that children would also not respond well to this treatment? Please think how it could feel if a dear man spoke of you so unwittingly before his peers or threatened you when you felt your worst. I doubt you would feel inspired, but we seldom cease thinking about how children feel about this treatment. We are accustomed to seeing children as less than novice, if in truth, that is what they are, inexperienced people doing their best to this point. How can we expect more?

If we want to create meaningful relationships with our children, we must modify the way we see them. The way we view at children, we need a major cultural transformation and that starts with you and me. We can assume they have good intentions, not negative intents. We can see the behaviour as communication rather than manipulation.

We must not give up our inner voices. Tune the society's cacophony and tune to your heart's whispers. It's not tyrants. They're not our adversaries. These are our valuable children.

Here's a freeing truth that I found out: It's all right to be tender. Love shouldn't truly be tough. Being

Tender does not open a child's door to walk through you. Tendering opens the door that your child can walk next to you. She hears the words that you say when she walks with you. You can guide her steps when you walk alongside her. The way to a connection is tenderness and connection is the key to parenthood. And everything starts with a fresh way of seeing our children.

We must also perceive parenthood in a new way if we are to see children in a new way. Instead of being the severe authoritarian (which is a position we perceive when we see a child doing terrible things), we can play the more linked role of teacher and guide. Instead of brutally chastising him (a task that we perceive necessary to make the child), we can be an encourager (because we understand he is already good).

Think about it. Think about it. The people who see past our mistakes and watch our beauty in our lives, those who see the light in us at times when we feel only the obscurity, are those who save us from the depths of blackness. These are the ones who help us to recognise again our beauty and light. Do you have someone like that in your life? All of us need this person.

The one who sees our light. -The one who sees our light. The one that reflects our light on us so that we can also see it. This is what a parent ought to be.

You might wonder how it works for me. How do my kids do that? Well, I'm not going to say they're perfect. I'm not going to say I'm either. But I don't know

They're going to say they're gorgeous people. My elder son borrowed money from his birthday and bought a gift from his brother. He answered, "I've got enough, and I simply want to have my brother happy." He supports a child in need via Compassion International and works to pay the sponsorship cost every month. He tells me that he wants all of them to be sponsored. Last Christmas, when I saw my stores stocked, but mine was empty, my two boys took it upon them discreetly to stock with handwritten love notes and the remaining Halloween sweets. This is hardly "sparkling, rude brats" behaviour.

You see some parents can assess achievement from spectators or clever rooms and finished task lists with qualities or comments of good behaviour, but I can measure success with love and compassion. I would say that positive parenting was clearly a success to date. Although my sons are good grades and "good behaviour," they have empathy and compassion, as I wish to send them into this world. The world needs more of that.

It's a safe sanctuary in our home. While my children sometimes argue, they quickly forgive and move on. They are the best friends, and I'm sure they'll always have their backs. You trust us. We trust them. We trust them. We're near and everybody knows that they're loved. I just can't ask more than that.

Questions for discussion

1. **How do you perceive about children? How does this view influence how you treat with them?**

2. **Do you feel the pressure for your children, especially in public, to behave like adults? Do you humiliate your infantile behaviour? Is their behaviour or your expectations the problem?**

3. **How do you speak to others in front of your children? Is it uplifting or crushing your words? It can be helpful to put your words through this filter before you speak: How would I feel if I came across?**

Put it in practise

It was the first big step in my way to positive parenting to change how I regarded my older son and his behaviour. Will you commit to be your child's one person who always sees and reflects her light? That starts by finding for positive intentions, even if she does something "bad."

When you see the motives of your child. You're going to get triggered negative. You can Get angry, ashamed, or upset, and you might be worried if you do not alter her that she will develop into a bad person

We're doing how we behave now. In that triggered condition, you may justify making the child feel bad, because in the long term you do it to make it better. So you scold her now, emphasise her character defects and make her feel bad about herself. Unfortunately she may assimilate this negative view into the self-konzept and regard herself as a bad person, because you reflect on the negative things you notice in her. We're acting like we see ourselves, thus it can turn into a vicious cycle.

But if you choose to view positive intentions, you understand that your child is not a bad person, but only needs direction on the matter. Although you continue to admonish her behaviour, your tone and behaviour are very different because of how you view her intention. Feeling that she is a good, positive person and has made a bad choice enables you to bring compassion into your correction, allowing her to do so without hurting her developmental self-conception.

Let's look at the identical scenario via two distinct views. Mason is coming and telling you that his sister, Mia, has spilt the red juice. Mia doesn't say she did! Her lips are red: you know she drank red juice.

Negative intention: She's a tiny sly liar! "You lie! You lie! I notice traces of juice on your mouth! Mason was honest. Mason was honest. Why wouldn't you be honest to me? In you, I'm terribly disappointed. Lying is wrong." It's wrong.

"Liar" isn't a moniker that you want to stick. If a child feels she's a liar, she's going to be a liar. Then she'll become a sneaky liar if she gets punished for being a liar. The prophecy of self-fulfillment! You created what you were afraid of.

Positive purpose: She doesn't want to go into trouble or deceive me. "Hmm. I envision red cherry lips. I appreciate your honesty. You had to drink juice

And it spilled accidentally? I drop things by accident sometimes. No big thing. No big deal. We only have to tidy things up. Come help me." Come help me."

Does the tone in such circumstances not feel significantly different? Probably the first one leaves Mia as an awful person. In the second she may feel a bit guilty about spilling the juice, but surely she is not shamed or berated. She purifies her mess, and everything is forgiven.

For a moment, let's focus our attention to Mason. For spilling the juice, he just "turned in" his sister. This is an opportunity to promote rivalry and strengthen tattling, which is what is happening in the first scenario. He receives the praise that he is honest. He might now look for new ways to convert his sister. Not only does she feel bad about herself, but I'd assume she feels angry about her brother, too. In scenario two, Mason only sees a problem solved. Since he sees problems to be solved, not punished, he doesn't learn any value in tattling.

Furthermore, there is no sibling rivalry, because Mason has been rejected from the talk with Mia.

Your task: look for the positive motives underlying the behaviour of your child. If you believe and transmit that you think she's a good person, she'll also believe she's.

How do you move from knee punishment to solution-oriented discipline?

Search the explanation for the behaviour first. Remember that behaviour is communication—it is an indication of a person's inner condition. We're working out how we feel, therefore kids who do bad probably feel bad inside. It may be so simple, like hunger or tiredness or a bigger question, like a problem with a friend or feeling separated from a loved one. The first question you should always ask is "what does this behaviour tell me?"

Secondly, please remember to discipline yourself before trying to discipline your child. An undisciplined parent cannot discipline a child properly. When you meet an out-of-control child, it causes a lot of turmoil and hurts that adds to the problem. It is best to wait till a sensible brain approaches the situation (that doesn't mean you are triggered and upset). It's all right to say, "I need a couple of minutes for myself, then we're going to talk about it."

Third, connect to your child by communicating your understanding—yes, your love. Connecting with a child is not a reward; it is a lifeline. He doesn't have to always get his way, but his love must always be his. Connecting does nothing to indulge children, to coddle or to spoil them. Connection does not give in. Connection does not give in. Underctandc connection.

Connection coddles not. The border is still there, but so is your love, which reassures a child out of control.

Fourthly, seek for a solution to the problem. Your child should be calm enough — connected with him — to get out of fighting or flying mode and think logically. Of course, this relies significantly on the child's age and maturity. A two-year-old cannot find a solution alone. For her, something simple might be like, "I'm not going to allow you hit your sister. Come sit by me. Come sit by me. A five year-old can start to provide ideas to fix the problem, but still needs some coaching. The following sentences are helpful for rolling the ball: "How will you fix that?" "We've got a problem. Can you think of a way to fix this problem?" She may need a push, but let her do most of her brain work. Children above the age of 8 may

Usually come up with a small solution, especially if they had practise. Just make sure it is followed through, regardless of the solution.

If your child refuses to come up with a solution and do so, your parental muscle will have to stretch by telling him your solution and making that he sees it pass. You may also have to do so if this isn't a new problem but a situation where the child knows the rules and a better solution, yet has made the wrong choice willingly.

Connected children are still children, and sometimes they also make awful decisions.

Restoration and reconnection are the last step. Restoration restores trust and reconstructs the notion of self. The goal throughout the restoration phase is to restore your child's self-worth feelings. He should come off the other side of the discipline always feeling that you think he's a good person, no matter how he slips occasionally. Reconnection comes through leaving the incident where it belongs and moving forward in good spirits in the past.

Summary of Soluble Discipline

Look behind the behaviour. Recall that behaviour is communication, therefore work out what the behaviour of the child communicates about its interior condition.

First discipline yourself. Wait until you are calm and sensible before the problem is dealt with.

Connect your child. Before the brain is free to learn what you wish to teach, the fundamental human needs of the love and connection must be met.

seek for a solution. Teach your child how to solve a problem. Teach her to correct her mistakes and to remedy relationships. This method is much better for her than simply 'making her pay.'

Restore the connection and reconnect. Make sure the authenticity of your child is recovered and she realises that mistakes are opportunities to learn and that a bad decision does not mean that she is a bad child. Reconnect by empathy and love and move on with good spirits, leaving the mistake in the past.

From Time-Out to Time-In

Toddlers and most pre-school children are not ready for problems in development. This is a function of the upstairs brain, which in young children is still very underdeveloped. This means that we have two main jobs when disciplining our own. One is to build and reinforce brain connections so that they can address the problem well in the future (we do this through teaching them to calm themselves and through repetitiously teaching the steps of problem solving). The second is to act as your brain on the ground, making rational choices until you are better able to do so.

Let's look at the conventional time-out method of discipline.

Recommended once we learned how harmful this practise was instead of spanking.

Did not know what the children needed and that separation was the most wounding experience of all. If we knew and comprehended that, we'd not use it as punishment." The fear of separation can stop the behaviour, so we think we have won. The desire to be good afterwards, however, comes from an insecure place, and this is the last place from which we want to come! What's more, when we punish a child by taking affection and warmth away and isolating him, we call on his reptile brain downstairs and activate this primary emotion of fear. The authors of No-Drama DICGIPLINE, Drs. Siegel and Bryson, call this "poking a lizard." It is far more useful to appeal to the upstairs brain. Finally, time-out typically gives children feelings of fear and aggression. Sitting in a chair for many minutes can stop a child's behaviour, but it doesn't help a child improve. We can't expect children to achieve better until we give them the instruments they need to succeed.

Time-in differs from time-out since the emphasis on first and second connection. Connection is what moves the brain upstairs.

Remember, logic and reasoning take place here. While still very underdeveloped, it is growing, and we may help her create a better brain through empathy and connection to a child. When we are

We show a child we get her, we understand the feelings and thoughts that inspired the behaviour, we understand. This does not mean that we accept the behaviour. Connection soothes activities in the lower brain and helps the child access her thinking brain, which she needs to understand the lesson she wants to teach. Children imprisoned in fear are not able to learn. After you connect and engage the upstairs brain, the child will be taught how to behave better.

Bring the child in the lap or "calm-down" in your home to employ the time-in.

When my kids were little, we had a calm-down area comprising books, a sketching pad, a smooth-down glitter jar (see 154), sensory rice and pop balls. I'd bring my child here and sit down with him for some peaceful activities. I knew his thought brain had returned online once he had ceased sobbing or fighting against me.

You can recognise when your child shifts from aggression or strong emotion to a condition of calm and receptivity. Once you perceive receptive, inform the child briefly what boundary she has breached and how she might modify her behaviour. For example, if she was crazy about needing a new cookie, you may say, "You have been upset about me, therefore you've screamed at me. Yet I'm not going to let you yell at me like that, but I understand you feel upset. Just like you don't like it, I don't like to be screamed at. The next time I'm upset, I want you to come to the relaxed area and sketch a picture to show me what you feel like."

This is where you need a paradigm shift. I know we have been indoctrinated to believe that we should be unloving or chilly towards children when they get mistaken, in order to show our disagreement. We think we motivate them to appear disgusting, tough tones, and time-bound isolation, but for the correct reasons this does not motivate children. In fact, if we remain caring and responsive even during correction, we build trust and attachment and children desire to be good for us thanks to this attachment. (Look up the six phases of Dr. Gordon Neufeld's attachment for more.)

Some people may be concerned about time-in being a reward for misconduct. We only view it a reward if we think we have to be disengaged to teach. Children only see it as a reward if they receive positive attention, which is not the case at home.

If you deal with several children at the same time, it's definitely a balancing act. I have for my boys two separate locations and I had merely to go

Between as I might best. It did not take long for my children to calm down with the items in their box. You will get there with consistency and patience!

Some children want to be alone when they get upset. Don't force a time-in if that's your child's preference. As long as the child can calm down and reach the sensible brain, wherever he does it does not matter. Just show that he needs it to be comfortable and remember constantly to wait and teach a calm brain.

More Punishment Alternatives

Remove it

I'm not a fan of eliminating rights or items solely to "make them suffer," but it is logical sometimes to remove an item. If my boys fight something, I can ask whether they can come to peace or whether they want me to step. If the conflict persists, I will take the item in my possession calmly and kindly. They heard me say, "Your relationship is more important than this item." They probably say it many times in their sleep. It's a message in which I wish to sink. Relations are of the utmost importance. Once the agreement is reached, the item is yours again.

My son once broke a limit on the use of his electronics.

I took that equipment away until we held a family meeting to discuss the problem and the possible remedies. We discussed Internet security and he wrote me a report on the need to keep within the boundary. Then I gave it back, and since then we have had no problems.

Table of Peace

This is a good alternative if you have older siblings or pals. Set a child-size table aside as the "peace table." Teach children to go to this particular place to settle an issue. I would recommend that you have on your table a feather known as a "talking feather." Anyone with a feather has the time to speak. The other child should listen without a break. When is the child?

She finished handing over the feather and talking to the point of view of the other child. Then you will talk to them about a solution until they can do it alone. Maybe it looks like this:

"I'm hearing Annie say she's upset because she was ready to use those blocks, and I'm hearing Beth say she was already using them and that she was not yet finished. Am I correct?" This kind of storey helps children to feel heard when they retell the facts of the dispute to them. "What is the solution possible? How about Beth when the blocks are finished, Annie let you know so you may use them? Annie? Is it going to work?"

Children must remain at the peace table until a peaceful solution is reached.

Take a pull over

Arguing in the car is a common and good complaint. For the driver, it's highly distracting. So I pull over on the side of the road when myself argues in the car and sit still. A few seconds later you are going to say, "Hey Mom, why have we stopped?" I say, "I can't focus with the two of you arguing on the road. When you've reached peace, I'll drive." I haven't had a lot of times to pull over. They caught up quite fast. This may not work for some children who are quite glad to continue on the side of the road. We must all figure out what works for our kids.

Write it down

Our values are obvious in the statement of our family mission and our rules are clear. And my boys are older, when a family rule breaks, I ask him to sit at the table and write down the rule that was broken. This helps him to remember it. Once the rule or value has been duplicated, I'll ask him to repeat to me. So if repairs are necessary for a relationship, possibly with his brother, another family member or a friend, I'll ask him how he wants to make a repair. If he needs my help, I

Just give it. Just give it. But that's something that I expect my two sons to do with little support.

Give thanks.

Regardless of how big a parent you are, your child will make mistakes. She's only human. Often we punish our children only because they're human and we're not always fully controlled by human emotions and behaviours, however we adults don't always totally control them either. Sometimes parents yell or slam a door out of irritation, and certainly we could do better, and should try to do better, but we aren't robots at the same time. Life is sometimes quite difficult and we lose it. We do not need someone to lecture us during this time, but someone to listen and understand, which is what children require many times. We should not keep children to a higher standard than we can achieve ourselves. Keep them high, but also be willing to give grace, if you can see that it is necessary. We all make mistakes and repeated correction will not stamp out the humanity of our children, nor will it stamp our own.

Stories of Success

I know that this significant transformation in how you discipline can first feel too big to stomach. You may feel that this is going to work for certain children, but not your own, or that a nonpunitive approach will lead to unruly children. I often receive notes from parents who are happy with the improvements made with positive, non-punitive discipline for children and families. I would like to share a few experiences from my readers with you to encourage you and to ease your mind in making this positive change.

Bailey wrote to me to share me how her non-punitive discipline works. "I am stunned to have made back at practically three of us without having to punish him at all. No timeouts. No timeouts. Don't sham or shout.

No physical or spanking punishment. He is indeed disciplined and taught with his dignity as a human being, and he is appreciated

It's not a brat! People like to be around him, and so are we. We enjoy him more than we ever thought possible and we like parenting.

Absolutely humiliating and outstanding.

Jessica is a member of my community on Facebook. She says, "I love how wonderful the advice is and how my family dynamics have changed. I'm one mother of three kids. Using the suggestions and strategies on this [Facebook] page, I could lead my children in a more healthier and happier way instead of bossing them. I now feel empowered and able to turn every fight, lie, misbehaviour, or explosion into a time of love and connection. That's invaluable to me."

Crystal's got to share a fantastic storey. I always love to hear from readers who have older children and have a positive relationship with them since I was young. She says, "We have utilised gentle parenting approaches, no punishment or rewards, never struck him or raised my voice under 10 times. We had a lot of discussion and fair limits. As a pre-school student, it was often hard to keep in mind that he should test and push boundaries. I've been working to keep the long-term goal in mind. Now, people always say to me that he is courteous, grateful and attentive. He is good at school and readily makes friends. Seriously, I never really need to talk about his behaviour since he does not misbehaviour and I think that is the foundation for respect that we set when he was younger. My advice is to keep doing what you know works and keep your long-term goals in mind. Now I watch my 11-year-old engaging with our toddler, and he uses the same tactics that we used with him. I love that with his tiny brother he's nice because he just repeats the way he is treated."

Rachel wrote to me about her success with time-out replacement. She explains, "I carry my son to his bed during a tanning and lie with him till he stops sobbing. I comfort and hold him. I soothe him. He calms down really fast. I ask if he's ready to talk about it once he's calm. I constantly wait for him to be ready. Hetells telling me why he's been upset. I listen and feel friendly. I listen. I also assist him verbalise if he has problems explaining his emotions. Then we talk about how next time we can do better. In our house this has done miracles. He answers this approach so much better. Now we don't normally reach to that point."

On my Facebook page, Mary shared her success with time in: "We started about a year and a half ago and she worked wonderful things about the amount of tanning as well as the duration of tension. It took a few months to begin seeing the effects, but it changed life!"

The tale of Jennifer is one I hope many more of you will hear. She explains, "Positive parenting has changed the dynamic of our whole family. I think it made me connect lot more positively with my hubby. We focus on the good in situations that allowed our children to see a healthy relation."

Finally, I need to share the comment Erica made with you: "Positive parenting, learning to be positive about the actions of my children, has not only changed my parenting, but has changed my whole heart for all men. For 15 years I've been doing this and I've got kids aged 1st, 15th, 18th and 20th. My older kids confirm that everyone who listens is different."

I welcome you to drop your success tales by my Facebook Positive Parenting: Toddlers and Beyond page. I love to hear from parents whose relationships with positive parents have been transformed. I look forward to hearing to you!

Chapter 11
RAISING EMOTIONALLY HEALTHY CHILDREN

Many of us learned to offer conditional love only. We have been raised to believe that unconditional love is soft and kids are spoiled and this idea is revolving around so many of our traditional parenting practises that we shouldn't be too gentle for children. There are all kinds of scary speculations about what can happen if we are "too easy" with them. It is tough for parents to tune all this noise and instead listen to intuition.

Again, I want to stress that positive parenting does not imply children are coddling, getting around their feelings to ensure they are not hurt or fail to set boundaries. The objective is emotionally healthy children, and unconditional love is crucial to emotional health and positive self-worth.

Psychologist Carl Rogers understood what he called UNGONDITIONAL pocious attention, or the necessity for unconditional love. He thought that childhood experiences are one of two key elements that shape the self-concept of a person. According to Rogers, we desire to feel and behave according to our image. He saw the child as having two fundamental needs: positive consideration and self-worth from others.

Rogers considers that a child of high view for him/her is well confronted with problems, accepts sometimes failure and unhappiness and is open with people, while a child of low self-worth avoids challenges, can't accept that life sometimes is unpleasant and defensive and protects people. Rogers thought that self-worth was initially derived from the relationships between the child and his mother and dad.

He also felt that we must be viewed positively by others. We must feel appreciated and respected, offer affection and feel loved. He made between unconditional and conditional positive consideration. Unconditional positive consideration is the unconditional love in which parents welcome the child entirely, and positive consideration is not withdrawn if the child accomplishes anything or makes a mistake.

In positive terms, the child receives approval only if it meets the expectations of the parents of behaviour. When she makes a mistake, the approval is removed. Therefore, the child is not loved for whoever it is but on the condition that it acts so that the parents are happy. 17

Since unconditional love and emotional wellness go along, I Believe it is time to reject normal procedures, which force us to remove love, affection and acceptance, and boldly step it into unconditional parenthood. I call that brave love because it takes bravery to fight the grain. To take a leap of faith requires guts. To break old routines, it takes bravery. The world needs brave parents who raise children who are emotionally healthy.

- **It's time to stand up to the**

- **It's time to rice up again that GLEARLY hurts us emotionally**

To our children. To our children. The recent trends, unfortunately, tend to move in the other way. Shaming and degrading children are praised as good parents in the name of discipline. We're talking hard against

Bullying in schools and on the Internet, but in our own homes. We acknowledge the significant mental damage and the connection to suicide caused by shame, humiliation and bullying by someone other than a parent

Yet it's still just child training for a parent, and for some reason that makes it okay.

It's not all right. We must release our worry that unconditional love will make them bad people if we commit ourselves to creating emotionally healthy people. To do so, it is important to see what it means to love without conditions, because I think we too frequently mix love with love without limits. It was perhaps believed that loving unreservedly meant that every behaviour is hugely allowed and not rectified. This is a fabricated view, fostered by the fearfulness that maintains us in high regard for hard love.

Unconditional love and correction is feasible and even necessary to coexist. Showing a child that your borders are fixed, consistent and unwavering demonstrates your leadership and respect.

Showing your love

The self-worth of a child is also stable, consistent and immovable. In addition to offering your child unconditional love, you may build your own self-worth in various ways. These comprise:

Showing bodily illness

Use positive body language as to how to lean in close proximity, gaze in his eyes when he says, smile, nod, thumb and high five

Using words of encouragement and praise and politely speaking to others about him

Give your undivided attention to connect and talk each day and warmly acknowledge him as he comes into a room creating a positive environment in which he is free to be who he is by creating close family ties and traditions, as well as participating in the community and in non-family groups such as Scouting, 4-Health, sport, etc. Ensure your expectations are consistent with your capacity and development stage

Creating a climate that enables him to express his ideas and feelings and to let him know that his responsibilities and independence are understood and respected

If your child displays signs of little self-esteem, begin building him daily with unconditional love and using the other ideas suggested in this chapter. Treat your mistakes as opportunities for learning and growing, learn your particular strengths, accept them as she is and communicate every day: "I love you, I see you, I believe in you, you matter." Here are several precautionary symptoms of low self-worth.

Prevents challenges Easily gives up nervous habits is typically withdrawn from other acts is extremely anxious or sensitive to thoughts of others makes unpleasant statements about themselves or others

The promotion of good self-esteem is part of parenting children who are emotionally healthy, but not the only factor. It is widely believed that experiences of childhood are crucial for emotional wellness. The same applies to the safe fastening. Family experiences can play an important impact. Positive family interactions and experiences foster good emotions. In well-adjusted families, positive communication is also an important aspect. This book addresses each of these areas, which means you are on a good way to raise an emotionally healthy child. Other elements that influence our mental wellness are education, outside social relationships, and genetic make-up.

Intentional parents make conscious decisions about the education of their child. Search all your possibilities and thoroughly analyse the benefits and disadvantages before making a selection. Besides the nearest public school, there are possibilities. Whatever you select, your child will thrive if you remain positive, supporting, encourage and keep open lines of communication.

Give him opportunities to participate in sports, voluntary work, clubs, art and music, where he can have positive social connection. Finally, teach your child emotional intelligence – the skills needed to detect and control one's own emotions and understand others' emotions.

To attain a child's full potential, she needs good emotional health. She must feel unconditionally cherished, respected and loved by her parents. We are self-worth builders, and we should always be aware of this reality. Leave behind practises that undermine the self-esteem of your child and learn how to help the parent to promote emotional health. Together, a generation of children who know how to be entire can be brought up if only we are brave enough to try.

Questions for discussion

- **What are your fears of unconditional love?**

- **Assess if your child has a positive or negative self value at the moment.**

- **Discuss what you are doing currently to build your child up or tear him down, and how you can improve it.**

Talk to your partner about ways of coexisting unconditional love and correctness. How, in particular, can you correct your child by saying "What you've done is wrong" instead of "Who you're wrong?"

Put it in practise

Since you started reading this book, you have put this chapter into practise. Good emotional health is one of the numerous benefits of positive parenting. Your emotional health is as important! Here are some suggestions to improve your emotional health.

- **Grow your friends circle. A support group of positive and encouraging people is important.**

- **Find your passion. Find your passion. Gardening, painting, collecting... What's yours?**

- **Pray and/or meditate and/or practise yoga. These stressors will improve your mood.**

- **Say no to over-engagement. It's just one of you! Don't try to do ten people's work.**

- **Stop self-criticism. Treat yourself to treat your child with kindness, respect and gentleness.**

Get involved in something that makes you feel good. Volunteer in an animal shelter or collect a food bank with the canned items. Helping others increases self-esteem.

Express optimism and thankfulness.

I'm not going to tell you to sleep plenty since this book might be thrown across the room. You are a relative. You're a parent. I get it. I get it. Try to sleep a bit.

One enjoyable way to increase the emotional intelligence of your child is by putting him in the mirror and asking him to make his faces in the following situations.

- Your ice cream cone has been dropped. (sad)

- You're on holiday. (enthusiastic)

- Your friend cannot come over. He can't come over. (disappointed)

- You hear a scary noise. (scared)

- Someone has grabbed away your toy. (anger)

- You open a gift.

- It's what you wanted! (surprised)

- Your shoes can't tie. (frustrated)

- For an hour you were running. (tired)

- Make yourselves!

Act action

Ask your child to act with situations that make her feel like this:

- Blessed

- Worried

- Sad

- frustrated

- Happy

- Angry

- Proud

- Embarrassed

- Disappointed

- Shy

- Nervous

- Tired

- Surprised

Conclusion

When you are an excellent parent, you are doing a huge service to your children, to your neighborhood, and to the whole United States. Your children who have not been mistreated or neglected are more likely to grow up to be healthy, happy, and productive citizens who will eventually become excellent parents themselves. Your family, as well as the families of your children, are more likely to be the strongest and most stable families in their respective areas.

Your abilities and dedication to your children also reduce the likelihood that your children will experience the academic, health, and mental health difficulties that so often predispose children to failure in school and a desire to retaliate against their peers. Therefore, you are also contributing to making communities safer and better places to live, as well as saving yourself and other taxpayers the expense of having to deal with public problems such as juvenile delinquency, substance abuse, school dropout, gangs, criminal activity, or violent crime and disorder.

You are also assisting in the improvement of educational institutions by sending them students who are prepared and capable of learning, and you are assisting civic and religious organizations by bringing them young people who are confident in their ability to help others as a result of the excellent care they have received themselves. As a bonus, you are contributing to the growth of the nation's economy since your well reared children are the most likely to have developed both the technical and interpersonal skills and outlooks necessary for success in the twenty-first century workforce.

Being a good parent in these fast-paced and chaotic times, on the other hand, is extremely difficult. There are both internal and environmental factors that contribute to the difficulty of becoming a parent. Included among these are the difficulties that so many parents face in getting along with one another in their marriages and other relationships, as well as external forces that result from children being pressured to use drugs and engage in adult sex at younger ages than ever before, pressures that put them at risk for becoming teenage parents and contracting potentially deadly STDs, among other things. There's also the issue of gangs, which may make leaving the house or apartment a dangerous endeavor, as well as the violence to which our children are exposed through the ubiquitous media and social media. Indeed, parenting at the dawn of the twenty-first century may be said to be parenting in the worst of circumstances....

However, as we have discovered, raising children in these difficult economic times is also parenting in the best of circumstances. At no other time in history have there been as many parenting support resources and programs available as there are right now. Furthermore, no previous generation of parents has had access to the Internet, which allows them to learn about services and programs that might be of support, as well as to enroll in and receive aid from these services and programs. The literally millions of parenting-related websites provide a veritable feast of educational possibilities. And, whereas previous generations might contact their local Information and Referral Service to find out where they could receive various services in their areas, there is now a single number that the great majority of American parents can use to get connected with local resources.

In addition, we now have substantial, research-based evidence on a productive pattern of parenting that best prepares our children to grow up to be healthy, happy, and productive adults in their own right. In order to follow this pattern, we must be warm, welcoming, and respectful of our children; firm and fair in our discipline; age-appropriate in our expectations for mature conduct; sensitive and attentive to our children's signs and needs; and a priority in our life for our children. Additionally, we now know from study that there are other patterns and even specific behaviors, like as corporal punishment and verbal violence, that are detrimental to our children's growth and well-being in general.

The best part is that there are now numerous programs and resources available to assist us in keeping our parenting in line with the productive pattern, including the contemporary parenting and family skill-building programs that we have heard about in the previous section. Our children benefit from these programs because they assist to teach in them the characteristics and values that are most highly regarded in our society, such as fairness and honesty; humility; politeness; mutual respect; empathy; compassion; hard work; responsibility; and self-discipline. The emphasis placed on relating to children without resorting to corporal punishment in these programs contributes to the advancement of the nonviolent philosophy.

In the 21st century, the combination of knowledge about what is most helpful in raising children in a democratic society, as well as the availability of numerous educational programs and resources to guide and assist us, makes the seemingly overwhelming problems of raising children not only manageable, but also surmountable.

The problem is to figure out how to make sensible and efficient use of all of the resources that are now so readily available to everyone. In addition, we may need to lobby in our local communities to guarantee that the entire range of contemporary parenting resources, including modern parenting and family skill-building programs, is available for our personal use as well as the use of our fellow parents, which is a problem in itself. Reading and using the presentation and principles included inside this book is an excellent beginning point, and you will be well on your way.

The "principles of positive parenting" are the underlying principles that underpin the various examples and guidelines for being a good and effective parent that we have discussed in this book. They are as follows:

- **In our everyday interactions with our children, as well as in our relationships with our partners and spouses, we set an essential precedent for what our children will learn and how they will behave.**

- **What we teach our children about positive and negative consequences whether they behave well or poorly is extremely important in determining how they will conduct themselves in the future. More often than not, these repercussions are of a good and caring kind, which increases the likelihood that our children will develop in a favorable manner. As a general rule, the more deliberate and time-consuming the consequences we offer when our children disobey, the more probable it is that our children will develop into prosocial and productive members of their communities.**

- **We need to adopt a non-hitting attitude and position in order to avoid serving as a role model for violence in the family. Such an attitude and approach encourages and demands us to acquire nonviolent problem-solving and conflict resolution strategies, such as those that are accessible in current skill-building programs, as well as to use them in our daily lives.**

Children must be given the attention and resources they need in our lives. This involves time, patience, sacrifice, and a desire to learn. Although time-consuming, it is well worth the effort since children whose needs are prioritized are more likely to grow up to be fine citizens as well as excellent mothers and fathers.

A Word of Encouragement

Greetings, parents.

It will take time and effort to establish your linked family. It is my recommendation that you not anticipate the entire process of parenting a person to be without hiccups. There will be traffic closures and detours in place. Troubles will come and go throughout the course of time. Being linked does not imply being perfect; rather, it entails loving one another despite our flaws and shortcomings.

Please keep in mind that while positive parenting requires you to be purposeful and to grow as a person, it does not need you to be perfect. You will not be the perfect parent or the perfect dad, and that is okay. Your children will not be perfect in every way. And that's just OK! Fortunately, all of the unconditional love and grace that your child receives as a result of your good parenting style is also extended to you as well. When you slip and fall, lift each other back up and continue on your journey together.

Keep a photograph of your child as a baby in a safe place at all times. When things get tough, remember to gaze at that image. When your child is exhausting you, when you feel like you can't handle another minute, take out the picture and stare at it for a moment.

When you look into those eyes on that first day, recall how it felt to be taken aback by the intensity with which they peered up at you and stole your breath away. The gorgeous eyes you gaze into now are the same as they were yesterday.

It's possible that your friends and family will disagree with your parenting decisions. They may believe you should be more assertive. They could believe you're pampering your youngster, and they're right. Rest confident that no one has ever had a bad outcome as a result of being overly cared for or protected. Forget about what they have to say and keep focused on your mission: creating a linked family of friends. There is no such thing as having too much love and care lavished upon you. Not for your partner, not for your children, but for yourself. Because none of us knows what tomorrow will bring, we should shower them with kindness on a daily basis.

Despite the fact that I do not have the answers to all of the questions that are posed to me, I do have a remedy for almost every difficulty in life: love. Your folks are wonderful.

Your husband and children are the ones that matter to you. Don't be afraid to show them how much you care. When a life is spent loving well, it is a life well lived. I assure you that you will never be sorry for expressing your affection.

Finally, some words of wisdom. In the evening, as you put your head on your pillow, ask yourself one simple question: Did my people go to sleep tonight feeling loved and valued? Take action if the answer is no. If the answer is yes, stand up and do something about it. Or, at the very least, decide to make tomorrow night's narrative a little different. Yes, my folks went to sleep tonight feeling loved and appreciated, so you may rest easy, lovely parent, knowing that you have done your job well. You're doing OK, thank you.